REVELATION

SATAN'S LAST VICTORY

All Scripture quotations in this book are taken from the King James Version of the Bible unless otherwise noted.

Revelation 13: Satan's Last Victory
Copyright © 2009 By Midnight Call Ministries
Published by The Olive Press, a subsidiary of Midnight Call, Inc.
West Columbia, South Carolina 29170

Copy Typists:	Lynn Jeffcoat
	Kathy Roland
Copy Editor:	Kimberly Farmer
Proofreader:	Kimberly Farmer
Layout/Design:	Michelle Kim
Cover Design:	Michelle Kim

Library of Congress Cataloging-in-Publication Data

Froese, Arno
      Revelation 13: Satan's Last Victory
      ISBN #9780937422663

      1. Bible—Prophecy   2. Antichrist

Printed in the United States of America

CONTENTS

Chapter 3
PROPAGANDA MINISTER OF ANTICHRIST 68

Chapter 4
WHEN GOOD IS BAD AND BAD IS GOOD 76

Chapter 5
THE GREAT UNIVERSAL CONFLICT   86

Chapter 6
THE GLOBAL POLITICAL MELTING POT 108

Chapter 7
ROMAN DOMINION 128

Part II
RACING TOWARD ECONOMIC GLOBALISM

Chapter 8
SATAN'S SUCCESSFUL SEDUCTION

Chapter 9
FOOTPRINTS OF SATAN   166

Chapter 10
THE BEAST OF PROSPERITY 188

Part III
RACING TOWARD RELIGIOUS GLOBALISM 203

Chapter 11
HOW ALL WILL BECOME ONE 204

Chapter 12
SATAN'S LAST VICTORY   222

Chapter 13
THE GREATEST TRAGEDY   232

REVELATION 13

R ecent developments have stunned the world. Something unprecedented has taken place: foreclosures, bank failures, factory closings, layoffs, economic downturn, etc. The financial elite, politicians and experts tried frantically to pinpoint the culprit, but without success. What is the reason behind it all? Scripture makes it clear to us: the world must become one. Unity—politically, economically, financially and religiously—will become a global reality. The things we are experiencing now are none other than a realignment of planet Earth, which will allow a new New World Order to solidify the nations of the world.

But there is a deeper reason. In the midst of the chaos, confusion and insecurity, it is the father of lies, Satan himself, who is preparing the manifestation of his rulership upon humanity.

This book reveals how the diabolical trinity will create a technologically advanced religion, the image of the beast, and a guaranteed prosperous life for everyone on earth through the mark of the beast.

What seemed virtually impossible a century ago is now becoming reality. A new global world order will be established, and all that dwell upon the earth will worship the dragon, the beast, and the image of the beast.

Revelation 13 is a compact unveiling of endtime events in Bible prophecy.

INTRODUCTION

R evelation 13 is one of the most fascinating and mysterious chapters in the entire Bible. This chapter is unique for our times because it does not identify countries defined by borders; rather, it speaks of the entire world—a global world. This message simply ignores that planet Earth is divided into five continents and into approximately 200 nations. It overlooks that these nations are diverse, speak different languages, live in different cultures, practice various religions, have their own customs, and celebrate their own holidays. Revelation 13 ignores all of it and simply reveals to us the final one world: a New World Order for all people on planet Earth.

We know that such a development was impossible only a century ago. The world was very diverse, divided by national borders, enforced by military powers. But in our days, something is happening that never occurred before: It is the race toward globalism.

At this point in time (9 March 2009), globalism has been placed on shaky ground as nations are desperately trying to take care of their own, and protectionism is becoming a serious issue for the world. But that is all temporary. We must never allow our view of Bible prophecy to be clouded by present circumstances. In the long run, the world will and must become one. That is the irrevocable statement of Bible prophecy.

Revelation 13 shows the epitome of the feigned success of Satan, the god of this world and the prince of darkness, who has subdued planet Earth through his deceptive devices. This chapter in the Bible speaks of politics, commerce and religion, all combined into one. The earthly authority is the Antichrist; his power is absolute. No one can exist on planet Earth unless he or she has the mark of the beast.

The 18 verses of Revelation 13 are a compact message about the end times, highlighting three major identities:

1. The dragon,
2. The first beast who is the Antichrist, and
3. The second beast who is the false prophet.

Trinity and Creation

The dragon, the first and the second beast, are the imitation of the Trinity of God. Their task is the creation of two specific things: 1. The image of the beast and 2. The mark of the beast.

While God created man in His image and commanded him to subdue the earth, the trinity of evil creates the image and the mark to subdue man. Satan's intent is to make man subject to his authority. Satan wants to be God. That, in brief, is the entire history of mankind.

Introduction to the Revelation of Jesus Christ

The message of this chapter has to be understood, studied and analyzed in context of the entire book of Revelation.

The book begins with, "The Revelation of Jesus Christ, which God gave unto him, to shew unto his servants things which must shortly come to pass; and he sent and signified it by his angel unto his servant John" (Revelation 1:1); and ends with, "The grace of our Lord Jesus Christ be with you all. Amen" (Revelation 22:21). It is therefore the Revelation of Jesus Christ.

The first three chapters reveal the exalted Lord and His messages to seven named churches. These churches are geographically and historically identifiable. They were real churches on the earth.

Opened Heaven

Then in chapter 4, something different happens: "After this I looked, and, behold, a door was opened in heaven: and the first voice which I heard was as it were of a trumpet talking with me; which said, Come up hither, and I will shew thee things which must be hereafter" (verse 1). The place of the event is now heaven. It specifically mentions that John was commanded to "come up hither" for the purpose of seeing and transcribing "things which must be hereafter."

Out of This World

When reading the book of Revelation, it is important to understand that this is a message from heaven. John is in the presence of the Lord in heaven. We are confronted with something that is literally out of the world, yet it is addressed to the people on the earth, particularly those who read and hear: "Blessed is he that readeth, and they that hear the words of this prophecy, and keep those things which are written therein: for the time is at hand" (Revelation 1:3).

Earthly Physical and Spiritual Physical

Reading the Book of Revelation as believers in Christ, we must ask for wisdom to distinguish between earthly physical things and spiritual physical things.

Here is an example: In chapter 1 we find a description of the Lord:

> And I turned to see the voice that spake with me. And being turned, I saw seven golden candlesticks; And in the midst of the seven candlesticks one like unto the Son of man,

21

clothed with a garment down to the foot, and girt about the paps with a golden girdle. His head and his hairs were white like wool, as white as snow; and his eyes were as a flame of fire; And his feet like unto fine brass, as if they burned in a furnace; and his voice as the sound of many waters. And he had in his right hand seven stars: and out of his mouth went a sharp twoedged sword: and his countenance was as the sun shineth in his strength (verses 12-16).

John is incapable of describing his observation, other than using metaphorical definitions to tell us what he sees. Notice the words "like" or "as." His hair was "as white as snow"; His eyes "as a flame of fire"; His feet "like unto fine brass, as if they burned in a furnace"; and His voice "as the sound of many waters." If we allow our imagination to roam, we come up with a twisted picture: a man with white hair, flames of fire come out of his eyes, his feet burning with fire, and his voice sounding like Niagara Falls. Such thoughts will deliver to us a totally wrong image of the spiritual truth the author tries to convey in the book of Revelation.

Let's look at another few examples.

Not Earthly Real

In chapter 5 we read these words: "...behold, the Lion of the tribe of Judah, the Root of David, hath prevailed..." (verse 5). In verse 6 we read: "...in the midst of the elders, stood a Lamb as it had been slain...." Quite obviously, the Lord has not become an animal, a lamb, neither has He become a lion. He is the one Isaiah describes: "For unto us a child is born, unto us a son is given: and the government shall be upon his shoulder: and his name shall be called Wonderful, Counsellor, The mighty God, The everlasting Father, The Prince of Peace" (Isaiah 9:6).

But again, we all would agree that a child could not be called "Counsellor, The mighty God, The everlasting Father, The Prince of Peace." From intellectual perspectives, it does not make sense. Thus we need to heed what 1 Corinthians 2:14-15 says: "But the natural man receiveth not the things of the Spirit of God: for they are foolishness unto him: neither can he know them, because they are spiritually discerned. But he that is spiritual judgeth all things, yet he himself is judged of no man."

The Seven-Headed Beast

It is equally unrealistic to assume that the beast we read of in Revelation 13 is an unknown animal that has seven heads and ten horns. If we allow such imaginations to enter our mind, seeing a picture of a monster, we will be hindered in understanding the realistic spiritual significance of this prophecy.

Revelation 13 may be difficult to understand, but that does not change what is written in 2 Timothy 3:16: "All scripture is given by inspiration of God, and is profitable for doctrine, for reproof, for correction, for instruction in righteousness." With these words, we receive the assurance of the Bible's reliability and instructions to carefully study the content of the Bible; in this case, the book of Revelation.

All the Earth

In particular, this chapter is applicable for our times because of the words identifying globalism: "all the world" (verse 3); "all kindreds and tongues and nations" (verse 7); "all that dwell upon the earth shall worship him" (verse 8); "the earth and them which dwell therein" (verse 12); and "them that dwell on the earth" (verse 12). These words clearly document our times. "All the world" means the entire world, and that is the manifestation of globalism.

It is self-evident that such could not have occurred 100 or 200 years ago. It was impossible for the world to unite, to be ruled by one leader, to have an economic system that monopolizes planet Earth. To think of a unified religion that would cause "all that dwell upon the earth to worship him" was out of the question.

The New Interdependence

Not too long ago, all nations were independent. Each had to look out for the security of its borders and establish new ones, mostly by force. Independently, they had to worry about their economy, finances and religion. Today, such is no longer the case. Virtually everything has become a global issue. Whatever happens in other countries affects ours. Independence has been replaced by interdependence. It stands to reason that such is necessary. When flying to Europe, for example, the U.S. has to have permission from Canada to fly into their air space. Think about landlocked countries such as Switzerland. What would happen if they could not fly in and out? Interdependence is a natural result brought about by technology.

Communication

Communication between the nations was limited. They spoke different languages. Translation was available only to the upper class. No one really knew what was happening in his or her neighboring country. Only that which the people were told by their respective leaders was the available knowledge to them.

Today, we are capable of communicating around the world at any time. Radio waves, telephone, satellites, and cables have interconnected the continents. Virtually everyone can communicate with anyone at any time.

Transportation

What about transportation? It was extremely limited before the 1900s. The only mode available was an animal: horse, donkey, camel, etc. This most uncomfortable mode of travel was also back-breaking, physically exhausting, and exposed one to great dangers. Even a king could not travel but a few kilometers a day. Besides, there were no paved streets that would allow one to travel in comfort. Outside a town or city, there were no paved roads, no concrete highways. Travel was subject to the weather. To go from one place to another, one could be stopped for several days because of rain, for example. There were only few bridges. In the heat of the summer, it must have been unbearable to travel the hot, dusty roads leading through dense woods with all kinds of dangers lurking around the corner. To travel across the oceans required a risky undertaking on a wooden ship, being at the mercy of the wind to move the ship, hopefully in the right direction. Stories about early seafaring travel are recorded for us in the book of Acts. Today, we can travel virtually around the world in about 24 hours. A 50 km (30 mile) drive around town is nothing unusual. Many do it on a daily basis.

Therefore, when we read in our Bible of a global political, economic and religious world society, we understand that only in our day are such things possible. We live in the time when these things can be fulfilled.

This brief introduction should set the stage for our studying of this particular chapter, Revelation 13, and drive the message home to our hearts that this indeed is the preparation for Satan's last victory!

PART I

RACING TOWARD POLITICAL GLOBALISM

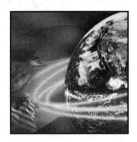

The Bible makes it clear that the world is doomed with the words, "...hasting unto the coming of the day of God, wherein the heavens being on fire shall be dissolved, and the elements shall melt with fervent heat?" (2 Peter 3:12). That's the indisputable and irreversible fact of the Word of God. Now science, as well, recognizes that the world as we know it cannot last indefinitely.

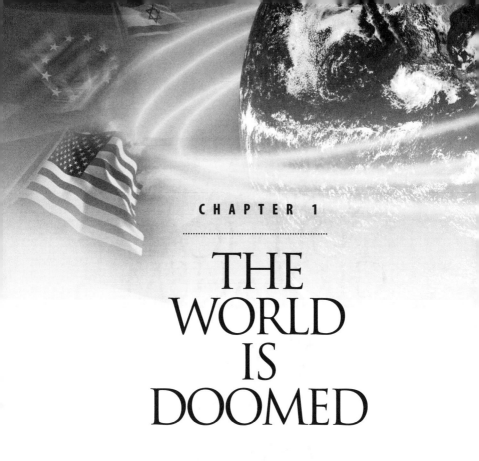

CHAPTER 1

THE WORLD IS DOOMED

The dragon, Antichrist and false prophet are in charge of planet Earth after the Church is removed with the Holy Spirit as the Comforter. Satan's aim is to deceive the world into believing that he has achieved peace, prosperity, and security for planet Earth, but in reality, the world is hopelessly lost. There is no future for planet Earth.

No Peace on Earth

Words in our vocabulary such as freedom, peace

and liberty are at stake in Revelation chapter 13. The world in general has been indoctrinated into believing that freedom is due to military force. That, however, is not the case, as we will learn later in our study. We are reminded of Revelation 6 where the Lamb opens the first seal, which reveals the rider on a white horse. This is a perfect picture of the deception of Antichrist. Then the second seal is opened, and verse 4 reads: "And there went out another horse that was red: and power was given to him that sat thereon to take peace from the earth, and that they should kill one another: and there was given unto him a great sword." Peace (freedom) is taken from the earth. Now Satan has a free hand. For the first time, the nations will know what peace and freedom is really all about.

The trinity of evil—the dragon, Antichrist and false prophet—has taken over planet Earth. Only one obstacle remains—the saints—but they are defeated.

The Dragon and the Two Beasts

The main identities in this chapter are the beast, the dragon and the other beast. We already named it the satanic trinity. They are the creators of two very important items: 1. the image and 2. the mark of the beast.

This chapter is extremely negative because these three identities are in charge of planet Earth. They do as they please; there is little to no opposition. That, apparently, is why we read in the previous chapter: "Woe to the inhabiters of the earth and of the sea! for the devil is come down unto you, having great wrath, because he knoweth that he hath but a short time" (Revelation 12:12).

The phrase, "the devil is come down unto you" is a significant statement. It reveals that there is no opposition from heavenly perspectives. It means that the time of grace has ended. The Church, which is the body of Christ, has been raptured into the presence of the Lord, and therewith the Spirit of comfort has been removed from the earth.

Holy Spirit Comforter

Recall the words of our Lord in John 14:16: "And I will pray the Father, and he shall give you another Comforter, that he may abide with you for ever." This promise was made before Pentecost.

It is important to understand that the Comforter (Holy Spirit) will have to be removed before Jesus comes. This is evident from John 16:7: "Nevertheless I tell you the truth; It is expedient for you that I go away: for if I go not away, the Comforter will not come unto you; but if I depart, I will send him unto you." In this case, Jesus could not send the Comforter while He was on earth; thus it stands to reason He cannot return to Earth until and unless the Comforter, which dwells in the Church, is removed from earth.

Someone may now ask, "If people are to be converted during the Great Tribulation, how is that possible if the Holy Spirit is not present?" Of course the

Holy Spirit is present; the Holy Spirit is God and God is omnipresent; but in the office as Comforter, the Holy Spirit is removed with the Church.

When we begin to analyze this from spiritual perspectives, we understand how horrible it will be for people on earth when the Comforter is removed, when "the devil is come down unto you." Then for the first time, the devil has a free hand and can do as he pleases. He no longer needs permission from God to act, because he is now harvesting the world, which has accepted him as divine. Nevertheless, his free exercise is time limited. This is evidenced in the last sentence of Revelation 12:12, "Because he [the devil] knoweth that he hath but a short time." During that short time, he is going to exercise his supreme power over all mankind.

Freedom and God's Grace

Unfortunately, many of us do not realize that the relative freedom we have in the civilized world is not due to our brave soldiers, but is exclusively due to the grace of God. Satan is not permitted to go above and beyond the principles of the Ten Commandments. For example, there is no government on earth that encourages their children to be disobedient to their parents or rewards lying, stealing, adultery and murder. These principles contained in the Ten Commandments are the foundation upon which all civilized nations are built on.

That is the reason why we are admonished to be subject to our prevailing government in Romans chapter

13. Every government, whether democratic, dictatorship, communist, socialist or monarchy, is ordained of God.

Verse 4 of Romans 13 says twice, "For he is the minister of God." Those who rule may be the devil's servants, but their limits of action are ordained of God. When the Church is gone, this limit will be removed; thus, Satan is going to have his heyday on earth.

We must add here that governments and leaders sometimes go beyond God's ordained limits. For example, Germany under Hitler. The Jews were to suffer persecution as indicated by Moses and the prophets, but mass murder of the Jews by the Nazis was beyond God's set limits. This is confirmed in Zechariah 1:15: "And I am very sore displeased with the heathen that are at ease: for I was but a little displeased, and they helped forward the affliction."

> *They are deceived into believing that there is hope —hope for peace and prosperity, hope for a better life, hope for a world without strife, without war and bloodshed.*

The World Is Doomed

This extremely negative chapter of the Bible also mentions the saints. Yet we read that they are defeated, "And it was given unto him to make war with the

34

saints, and to overcome them." Quite frankly, this is one of the most hopeless verses in the Bible. If only humanity would realize the hopeless situation they find themselves in! But they are deceived into believing that there is hope—hope for peace and prosperity, hope for a better life, hope for a world without strife, without war and bloodshed—but such hope is vain according to Holy Scripture. The conclusion is crystal clear: The world collectively is hopelessly lost! It is doomed.

My son Joel put a book on my desk titled *Decoding the Universe*. Here is what it says in the Introduction on page 1:

> Civilization is doomed.
>
> That's probably not the first thing you want to read when you pick up a book, but it's true. Humanity—and all life in the universe—is going to be wiped out. No matter how advanced our civilization becomes, no matter if we develop the technology to hop from star to star or live for six hundred years, there is only a finite time left before the last living creature in the visible universe will be snuffed out. The laws of information have sealed our fate, just as they have sealed the fate of the universe itself.

The author of the book, Charles Seife, did not get his information from the Bible, but from available science. Civilization is doomed that is his conclusion.

Eternally Saved or Doomed

But there is an option. Here is what the Bible says

about the future: "Looking for and hasting unto the coming of the day of God, wherein the heavens being on fire shall be dissolved, and the elements shall melt with fervent heat? Nevertheless we, according to his promise, look for new heavens and a new earth, wherein dwelleth righteousness" (2 Peter 3:12-13). Yes, civilization is doomed, but not for those who believe. Satan's attempt to destroy God's plan of salvation will utterly fail. It will end not only in the greatest catastrophe ever for him and all who reject God's offer of free salvation in Christ Jesus, but it will be eternal. This is made clear in Revelation 20:10: "And the devil that deceived them was cast into the lake of fire and brimstone, where the beast and the false prophet are, and shall be tormented day and night for ever and ever."

In contrast, we have the wonderful promise in the next chapter: "And he that sat upon the throne said, Behold, I make all things new. And he said unto me, Write: for these words are true and faithful" (Revelation 21:5).

SATAN'S MASTER DECEPTION

The beast that rises out of the sea is the Antichrist. He is Satan's masterpiece. The world receives him as the greatest benevolent leader ever to come on the scene. People love and adore, even worship him, but his characteristics are revealed to be the epitome of blasphemy.

The First Beast

"And I stood upon the sand of the sea, and saw a beast rise up out of the sea, having seven heads and ten horns, and upon his horns ten crowns, and upon his heads the name of blasphemy" (Revelation 13:1).

We will now take a closer look at the three identities we already mentioned briefly: the dragon, the beast, and the second beast.

How are we to understand the statement, "a beast rise up out of the sea"? First of all, the sea cannot be identified by geography as can land. Here is an illustration: When raindrops fall into the sea, they become identified with that body of water. Actually, those drops of water lose their identity. Therefore, when we read that the first beast comes out of the sea, it means he comes from a geographically unidentified area. That should suffice for us not to speculate as to the location from which the Antichrist will arise. Most scholars understand the sea to represent the masses of the people.

Blasphemy

What is "the name of blasphemy"? There is no direct reference to the name or words that constitute blasphemy, but we may speculate. The name could be "Jesus Christ, the Messiah of Israel and the Savior of the world." This may shock many who think that blasphemy must be something extremely negative. However, if Satan can successfully present his man as the Savior of the world, would that not be the perfect demonstration of blasphemy?

We have to remind ourselves that the first beast, the Antichrist, is the epitome of Satan's master deception. He is the one Jesus speaks of when He said: "I am come in my Father's name, and ye receive me not: if another shall come in his own name, him ye will receive" (John 5:43).

The Priestly Connection

The Antichrist is the copy of God's intention with mankind. God wants to save. He shows His way through the office of the priest. The priest represents the people to God. We read in Exodus 28:36: "And thou shalt make a plate of pure gold, and grave upon it, like the engravings of a signet, HOLINESS TO THE LORD." Where was this golden signet engraved with the words "HOLINESS TO THE LORD" placed? "Upon Aaron's forehead" (verse 38). The holiness of the priest's office was made visible by this golden signet, ordained by God. Aaron would visibly demonstrate that God had elected him to be holy for His holiness.

> *Thus the holy name of our most holy and exalted Lord would be the perfect one to be placed upon the most abominable creature, the Antichrist.*

We may also utilize 2 Corinthians 3:2 to show the invisible ordained priesthood of the believer: "Ye are our epistle written in our hearts, known and read of all men."

Thus the holy name of our most holy and exalted

40

Lord would be the perfect one to be placed upon the most abominable creature, the Antichrist. That could be the climax of blasphemy against God.

Satan's aim is to be God. He wants to be made the object of worship. Here we must recall the event recorded in Matthew 4:8-10: "Again, the devil taketh him up into an exceeding high mountain, and sheweth him all the kingdoms of the world, and the glory of them; And saith unto him, All these things will I give thee, if thou wilt fall down and worship me. Then saith Jesus unto him, Get thee hence, Satan: for it is written, Thou shalt worship the Lord thy God, and him only shalt thou serve."

This is the Devil's World

Contrary to popular belief and what is propagated within Churchianity, the nations of the world are not the nations of God, but are actually of the devil. The offer the devil makes to Jesus is his legitimate right: "All the kingdoms of the world, and the glory of them...will I give thee, if thou wilt fall down and worship me."

Someone may now object and say the Lord is the God of the world: He is the supreme ruler over heaven and earth. Psalm 22:28 says, "For the kingdom is the LORD'S: and he is the governor among the nations." That indeed is true, but God is not unrighteous; He cannot contradict Himself, and He cannot overlook sin. His righteousness requires Him to judge and destroy sin. The Word of God says, "He that committeth sin is of the devil" (1 John 3:8). Since there is no one without sin, all are legally placed under the authority of Satan. Hence, this is the devil's world.

Limited Authority

Maybe a word of explanation is appropriate. The devil, who is the god of this world, does not have unlimited authority. He cannot do as he pleases in all instances; he is subject to the ultimate authority of God. We already mentioned that if God would withdraw His grace and give Satan free will, then indeed we would experience hell on earth literally. Only when God's boundaries are removed, the second part of Revelation 12:12 will be fulfilled: "Woe to the inhabiters of the earth and of the sea! for the devil is come down unto you, having great wrath, because he knoweth that he hath but a short time."

Satan's Aim

Again, what is the dragon's aim? Answer: to produce a diabolically inspired person and present him to the world as the savior. "Who opposeth and exalteth himself above all that is called God, or that is worshipped; so that he as God sitteth in the temple of God, shewing himself that he is God" (2 Thessalonians 2:4).

In God We Trust?

When we begin to understand this fact, we come to a very unpleasant truth that concerns each of us. The truth is that the god of this world is not Jesus Christ the Crucified. We may proudly proclaim, "In God We Trust or "One Nation Under God," but it is not Jesus the Crucified. It is the imitation; it is the god of this world. It is blasphemy.

The god of This World

How can we recognize Satan's deception? The answer is revealed in the word "we." Who are "we"? Quite obviously, we mean the people of the United States of America. That, however, causes a conflict, because that little word "we" includes a variety of people: unbelievers, atheists, members of various cults and false religions, even blasphemers. Realizing this fact, we as believers in Jesus Christ cannot be identified with this "we" group. Please allow for the possibility that those slogans are part of blasphemy.

In America, we are particularly sensitive to this issue, and the majority seems to assume that the "God and country" issue is limited to the U.S.A., but that is far from the truth. Virtually all nations on planet Earth are influenced to the same degree. After all, there is only one Satan; he is the same in all countries. Many people think that the inclusion of biblical references or names such as "God," "Almighty" or "Jesus" somehow automatically sanctifies that nation and sets it apart from the rest of the world. But believing such is the demonstration of the success of deception of the real deceiver, the father of lies, Satan.

The following chart illustrates how nationalistic many of the nations of the world are:

Ranking of General National Pride between 1995-96 and 2003-04

Ranking of General National Pride between 1995-96 and 2003-04			
	Rank		Change in score
	1995-96	2003-04	
Austria	1	3	-0.14
United States	2	1	0.50
Australia	3	2	0.47
Hungary	4	5	0.34
Canada	5	4	0.47
The Philippines	6	8	0.20
New Zealand	7	7	0.16
Japan	8	10	-0.49
Ireland	9	12	-0.97
Spain	10	8	0.52
Slovenia	11	9	0.12
Norway	12	16	-0.88
Poland	13	13	-0.49
Great Britain	14	14	-0.23
Russia	15	11	0.39
Sweden	16	20	-0.42
Czech Republic	17	15	0.75
Latvia	18	21	-0.47
Germany-West	19	17	0.88
Germany-East	20	19	0.59
Slovakia	21	18	0.93

Source: "National Pride in Cross-national and Temporal Perspective," by Tom W. Smith and Seokho Kim, NORC, University of Chicago. Published in *International Journal of Public Opinion Research,* 18 (Spring 2006): 127-136

The Animalistic Nature

"And the beast which I saw was like unto a leopard, and his feet were as the feet of a bear, and his mouth as the mouth of a lion: and the dragon gave him his power, and his seat, and great authority" (Revelation 13:2). When we read these words, we are immediately reminded of Daniel 7:4-6:

> The first was like a lion, and had eagle's wings: I beheld till the wings thereof were plucked, and it was lifted up from the earth, and made stand upon the feet as a man, and a man's heart was given to it. And behold another beast, a second, like to a bear, and it raised up itself on one side, and it had three ribs in the mouth of it between the teeth of it: and they said thus unto it, Arise, devour much flesh. After this I beheld, and lo another, like a leopard, which had upon the back of it four wings of a fowl; the beast had also four heads; and dominion was given to it.

In Revelation, the animals are enumerated in the reverse direction: first the leopard, then the bear, and lastly, the lion. But where is the fourth beast? It is not mentioned, because the fourth beast is Satan incarnate.

Man Becomes Beast

Daniel 7:7 reads: "After this I saw in the night visions, and behold a fourth beast, dreadful and terrible, and strong exceedingly; and it had great iron teeth: it devoured and brake in pieces, and stamped the residue with the feet of it: and it was diverse from all the beasts that were before it; and it had ten horns." The beast himself is the fourth beast, which is not identified with any animal. There is no problem identifying the lion (Babylon), the bear (Persia) and the leopard (Greece), but the last one is the ultimate success of Satan: man becomes beast and beast becomes man.

Satan's Power

Something unique is revealed in Revelation 13 verse 2, namely, "the dragon gave him his power, his seat, and great authority." Gave it to whom? The beast that came out of the sea. This could not be said for the lion, the bear and the leopard. They did not receive their power from Satan. The three previous Gentile superpowers were identifiable; they could be compared to these three animals, while the fourth is a product we may define as "out of this world."

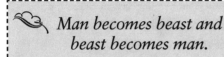

Man becomes beast and beast becomes man.

The Beast Receives

Also, we recognize that the beast apparently has nothing to show of his own merits; he receives his power, position and authority from the dragon. Who is the dragon? The explanation is given in chapter 12, verse 9: "And the great dragon was cast out, that old serpent, called the Devil, and Satan, which deceiveth the whole world: he was cast out into the earth, and his angels were cast out with him." Here we have the originator of sin defined by a fourfold title:

1. The great dragon,

2. The old serpent,
3. The Devil and
4. Satan.

This is one and the same identity, and he is the one who gives authority and power to the beast.

The Imitator

This is again a copy of the words of Jesus: "Then answered Jesus and said unto them, Verily, verily, I say unto you, The Son can do nothing of himself, but what he seeth the Father do: for what things soever he doeth, these also doeth the Son likewise" (John 5:19). Thus we see the first beast, the Antichrist, is the imitation of the Son of God. He has nothing; all things are given to him by the dragon, that is, Satan. The second beast is distinctly different: he is the false prophet. We may call him the imitation of the Holy Spirit. We will deal with him in more detail later on.

Global Power

"And I saw one of his heads as it were wounded to death; and his deadly wound was healed: and all the world wondered after the beast" (Revelation 13:3).

It seems that most scholars identify the beast and the system of the beast as the continuation of the Roman world empire. When seven heads and ten horns are mentioned, it is assumed that this speaks of the rulers of the Roman Empire. However, this theory requires the Antichrist system to be localized, primarily in Europe and the Middle East. But the Bible says, "all the world."

While we clearly recognize that the beast is a person, a man, we also understand that this is much more. His manifestation with seven heads and ten horns, is not limited within the geographical boundaries of the Roman Empire, but is worldwide. This speaks of a global system in which all the people of the world are involved.

I think it to be a mistake when we isolate this personality to one place such as Rome. Some scholars identify the beast system with the Roman Catholic Church. By supporting such an interpretation, we totally ignore the masses of people under the authority of different religions such as Islam, Hinduism, Buddhism, etc. It is definitely not just the Roman system that is described here, but all other religions as well. It is truly global. In our introduction, we already highlighted several Scriptures to document that all the earth, the whole of the planet is involved.

The Seven Heads

While this last kingdom, empire or system is global, there is a geographical earthly contact. This is what we read in Revelation 17. It speaks of Mystery Babylon the Great, the mother of harlots and abomination of the earth. This woman sits upon the seven-headed beast: "And the angel said unto me, Wherefore didst thou marvel? I will tell thee the mystery of the woman, and of the beast that carrieth her, which hath the seven heads and ten horns" (verse 7). Who are the seven heads? Verse 9 answers: "And here is the mind which hath wisdom. The seven heads are seven mountains, on which the woman sitteth."

Who is the woman? Again, we have the answer in this chapter: "And the woman which thou sawest is that great city, which reigneth over the kings of the earth" (verse 18). The seven heads are seven mountains, and the woman is revealed as "that great city."

There are a number of cities built upon seven hills. Jerusalem is one, but the most famous is Rome. Also, we cannot deny that Rome was the decisive political religious power during the time of Jesus and the apostles, and Rome is identified as the final Gentile power structure. It is global: "which reigneth over the kings of the earth."

Therefore, I venture to say that Satan's point of contact with the nations of the world is Rome, while God's point of contact is the city of Jerusalem. There outside the walls, the Lord Jesus Christ was crucified on Golgotha's cross, pouring out His life in His blood for the remission of sins of all who believe.

From one city comes success, from the other blessing. From one comes pride, arrogance and riches, and from the other humility, servitude and death. From one comes eternal damnation, and from the other eternal salvation.

If we keep these two points in mind, we should

receive a clearer picture of prophecies as we find them written, particularly in the book of Revelation.

Demonic Earthly Contact

John was called up into heaven, and he reports to us something that is out of this world. He sees the past, present and future all in one. He sees a person and a system controlled by the prince of darkness, the god of this world. I propose, therefore, that the

> *The seven heads, including the one that is wounded unto death, are representative of the power structure of the demonic world.*

seven heads, including the one that is wounded unto death, are representative of the power structure of the demonic world. The beast, however, the Antichrist, is the contact person on earth. His power becomes manifested visibly, because the people on earth are apparent witnesses of this miraculous restoration of healing. Therefore they are full of excitement, joy and exaltation about this beast.

Political Worship

"And they worshipped the dragon which gave power unto the beast: and they worshipped the beast, saying, Who is like unto the beast? who is able to make war with him?" (verse 4). This is devil wor-

50

ship. They worship the dragon who gives power to the beast. Here we have demonstrated the unity between politics and religion. They are solidly united; they have become one. This again is an imitation of God the Father, God the Son, God the Holy Spirit, and His Church. Remember the words of Jesus in John 17:23: "I in them, and thou in me, that they may be made perfect in one."

Satan must produce a copy of this perfect oneness.

Worshiping Man

It seems unreasonable to assume that the people of the world will actually worship a man who is called the beast. Indeed, I would agree with that conclusion, looking at this statement from a shallow point of view. But in contemplating this prophecy and comparing it with today's world, it no longer seems unreasonable.

In English speaking countries, the Queen of England is well known. Whenever she appears, people will stand in line for hours just to get a glimpse of this woman. Yet she is no different from any other woman; she is a sinner in need of salvation.

How about film stars? People pay great sums of money to own a piece of clothing worn by an actor. The sports world has its idols too. An athlete who wins an Olympic gold medal can sell him or herself to a promotions firm. Millions upon millions will buy that product because their athlete endorses such.

If a person spends an exorbitant amount of money to attend an appearance of a celebrity, or stands in line for hours just to see or touch that celebrity, then I would allow for the possibility that such behavior constitutes worshiping that particular celebrity.

Deception by Imitation

We must keep in mind the two words, "imitation" and "deception." The people of the world do not realize that they are deliberately participating in devil worship. Rather they think it is Jesus, the Son of the Living God, who has manifested Himself through these various religions and now has taken control of planet Earth. That is the deception.

The Apostle Paul warns us about this deception: "For if he that cometh preacheth another Jesus, whom we have not preached, or if ye receive another spirit, which ye have not received, or another gospel, which ye have not accepted, ye might well bear with him" (2 Corinthians 11:4). Here Scripture documents the existence of another Jesus, another spirit and another gospel.

Why do people follow the false instead of the genuine? The answer is one word, deception. The details on how this deception is implemented are recorded in 2 Corinthians 11:13-15: "For such are false apostles, deceitful workers, transforming themselves into the apostles of Christ. And no marvel; for Satan himself is transformed into an angel of light. Therefore it is no great thing if his ministers also be transformed as the ministers of righteousness; whose end shall be according to their works."

Politics and Religion

When we begin to understand that this deception scheme has been in progress for about 2,000 years, we see this extremely dangerous development in a clearer light. Religion, as is evidenced, combined with politics and the love of money, is in our days the most powerful tool of deception.

Churchianity here in America fights desperately to keep their religious identity in government. The Vatican too continuously urges the European Union politicians to keep the "Christian heritage" of Europe in its constitution. Catholicism insists that politics and religion must be married. Evangelical Christianity today proclaims the same message.

> *Churchianity here in America fights desperately to keep their religious identity in government.*

Christian Nation

History documents that virtually all declarations for hope and prosperity for the future were expressed with words of religious substance by politicians.

Many scholars and authors have tried desperately

53

to picture the United States of America as a Christian identity. Words and sentences of the Founding Fathers are picked out randomly to make it look as if the country was established as a Christian nation. But there is a problem. When we take a closer look, we find that most, if not all of these

> *The truth is that the Bible makes absolutely no provision for the establishment or existence of any Christian nation.*

words were spoken and written by people who had no personal faith in Jesus Christ. Most of the founding fathers were Deists who conveniently used Scripture for their political aims. About 30 percent of the signers of the Declaration of Independence were members of the occultic Freemason religion.

If we check other nations, particularly European ones, we find that they too very liberally used words such as God, blessing, Jesus, Almighty, Holy Scripture, etc. in their political proclamations. The truth is that the Bible makes absolutely no provision for the establishment or existence of any Christian nation.

Finally Peace

The worshiping of the dragon and the beast, which we read of in verse 4, is the result of the people of the world believing they have attained what they had hoped and prayed for. Finally, there is peace and prosperity; there is a man who makes sense. He speaks words precisely how they like to hear them. But those good-sounding words originate with the dragon, the father of lies, the great deceiver, the murderer from the beginning.

The Benevolent Leader

The beast is an absolutely unique personality, greatly beloved throughout the world; thus people exclaim, "Who is like unto the beast?" He has no equal; he is the final, benevolent leader of the world. No one is better, and none has a chance to oppose him. He is the absolute number one, the superhero of the world.

> *The Antichrist will make use of well-respected religious vocabulary, such as people would gladly accept.*

"And there was given unto him a mouth speaking great things and blasphemies; and power was given unto him to continue forty and two months. And he opened his mouth in blasphemy against God, to blaspheme his name, and his tabernacle, and them that dwell in heaven" (verses 5-6).

Again, we must keep in mind this is a report from heaven, giving details of events taking place on earth. This does not mean that Antichrist is using vile lan-

55

guage or cursing God. The opposite is true. The Antichrist will make use of well-respected religious vocabulary, such as people would gladly accept. Nevertheless, it is still blasphemy, because he is not Christ but Antichrist. He will act righteously, but he is the epitome of unrighteousness.

Biblical Righteousness

Let's look at a biblical example that deals with man's righteousness. We all know the saying, "there is a little bit of good in every man." We are taught that man is noble and tries to do the right thing. We honor people who have achieved things to benefit our nation and the world. We call them heroes or righteous ones. But what does the Bible say? "But we are all as an unclean thing, and all our righteousness are as filthy rags; and we all do fade as a leaf; and our iniquities, like the wind, have taken us away" (Isaiah 64:6). This is not speaking about our failures, our sins, but it speaks of our very best, our righteousness. Honorable citizens—those who take care of their family, do no evil unto others, go to work faithfully, and pay all bills and taxes—are considered praiseworthy and righteous, but when it comes to God's righteousness, their deeds are placed into one category: filthy rags.

More Blasphemy

We have no record of what words the beast is

speaking that are defined as blasphemy. But we know the direction: the words are aimed against God, His name, His tabernacle, and the residents of heaven. Blasphemy does not necessarily constitute cursing God and the Bible. After all, the Bible is a relatively well-known document for the people of the world, and surely they would not want to have their religious beliefs offended. The Antichrist, according to these Scriptures, will support Churchianity; he will speak well of religion in general and Christianity in particular. Antichrist is the imitation of our Lord Jesus Christ. He will demonstrate to the people of the world that he has established his kingdom of peace on earth. He is the power behind the success of the global world. He will proclaim "peace on earth, good will toward men." He is the savior; he is the god who turned this dangerous world into a paradise by his own power.

One may imagine that he will use the Scripture and openly challenge the saints: Where is your God? Where is your heaven? Where are those who can oppose me? I am god, I am the creator of heaven on earth, I am the savior of the world, I am he who has brought peace to planet Earth!

Let us again read the words found in 2 Thessalonians 2:4: "Who opposeth and exalteth himself above all that is called God, or that is worshipped; so that he as God sitteth in the temple of God, shewing himself that he is God." That is the epitome of blasphemy!

Blasphemy: Unforgiven Sin

An event recorded in Mark 3 reveals blasphemy as the unforgiven sin: "Verily I say unto you, All sins shall be forgiven unto the sons of men, and blasphemies wherewith soever they shall blaspheme: But he that shall blaspheme against the Holy Ghost hath never forgiveness, but is in danger of eternal damnation: Because they said, He hath an unclean spirit" (Mark 3:28-30). The blasphemy the scribes in Jerusalem committed was expressed in their sentence: "He hath Beelzebub, and by the prince of the devils casteth he out devils" (Mark 3:22). They gave credit to the devil instead of to the Holy Spirit. Likewise, the beast, who will have some opposition, will contradict the saints with the statement that they are the devil's servants. The Antichrist is the one presented to the world as the real Christ, but he is in reality a substitute, the false Christ.

Saints Defeated

Here are the enemies of Satan: "And it was given unto him to make war with the saints, and to overcome them: and power was given him over all kindreds, and tongues, and nations" (verse 7). Who are the saints? Doubtless, they are the ones who do not follow the gospel of the Antichrist. Some of these saints are identified in Revelation 6:9-11:

> And when he had opened the fifth seal, I saw under the altar the souls of them that were slain for the word of God, and for the testimony which they held: And they cried with a loud voice, saying, How long, O Lord, holy and true, dost thou not judge and avenge our blood on them that dwell on the earth? And white robes were given unto every one of them; and it was said unto them, that they should rest yet for a little season, until their fellowservants also and their brethren, that should be killed as they were, should be fulfilled.

These are the martyrs who were killed because they kept the testimony of Jesus.

We learn from verse 7 that Antichrist overcomes the saints; that means they are defeated. Subsequently, the warning is given to the saints for patience and faith. They witness diabolical unrighteousness, and are urged not to participate in it.

More Saints

In chapter 7 of Revelation, there is a group of saints who are sealed by God in their foreheads: 12,000 of each tribe of the children of Israel, thus 144,000. After listing the twelve tribes, verse 9 reads: "After this I beheld, and, lo, a great multitude, which no man could number, of all nations, and kindreds, and people, and tongues, stood before the throne, and before the Lamb, clothed with white robes, and palms in their hands." These saints will be confronted with Antichrist and his power. The tribulation saints, as they are generally called by Bible scholars, are at the mercy of the Antichrist system. Their very physical existence is put on the line.

Chapter 14, verse 12 states: "Here is the patience of the saints: here are they that keep the commandments of God, and the faith of Jesus." They keep their faith in Jesus instead of faith in the new global system, where the false Jesus rules supreme.

Jewish Saints?

The 144,000 saints are Jewish. The innumerable multitude is definitely Gentile. Revelation 12:17 clearly identifies the Jewish saints: "And the dragon was wroth with the woman, and went to make war with the remnant of her seed, which keep the commandments of God, and have the testimony of Jesus Christ." Who is this woman? She is identified in chapter 12, verse 5: "And she brought forth a man child, who was to rule all nations with a rod of iron: and her child was caught up unto God, and to his throne."

"A Place Prepared of God"

From Israel, the Lord came forth. He proclaimed, "...salvation is of the Jews," and He will rule the nations of the world "with a rod of iron." We should also read chapter 12, verse 6: "And the woman fled into the wilderness, where she hath a place prepared of God, that they should feed her there a thousand two hundred and threescore days."

The woman represents Israel, and she will be protected by God in "a place prepared of God." Where is this place? Many respectable Bible scholars point to Petra in Jordan, but that does not correspond to the statement we have just read, "a place prepared of God." Those who have been there know that the place called Petra is a perfect death trap. Once they are in, they cannot get out. Just a few bombs would totally annihilate all of Israel's population.

We have to stick to Holy Scripture, and not use our imaginations to come up with a private interpretation. This is a place "prepared of God"; it is the wilderness. Verses 14 emphasizes, "She is nourished for a time, and times, and half a time"; that is, for three-and-a-half years. Doubtless, this is God's supernatural intervention to insure Israel's survival. Thus we can be assured, there will be great numbers of Jews who will believe in Jesus, because they recognize that the Gentile world is worshiping Satan.

Global Worship

Then we read: "And all that dwell upon the earth shall worship him, whose names are not written in the book of life of the Lamb slain from the foundation of the world" (Revelation 13:8).

Note here the words, "all that dwell upon the earth." This plainly speaks of the entire world. The only exceptions are those whose names are written in the Book of Life of the Lamb.

Which Book of Life?

What is the Book of Life? My understanding is that there are two Books of Life. One speaks of our present life in flesh and blood, while the other speaks of our eternal life, and that is the Book of Life of the Lamb.

Take Moses, for example. He prays to God: "Yet now, if thou wilt forgive their sin—; and if not, blot me, I pray thee, out of thy book which thou hast written" (Exodus 32:32).

Moses is putting his life on the line for his people. We have to understand that he worked diligently for the people of Israel. He defended an Israelite against an Egyptian, killed the Egyptian, and hid him in the ground. As a result, he became a fugitive for 40 years. Then God told him to go back to Egypt and tell Pharaoh, "Let My people go." Finally, the people went out. Great and mighty signs accompanied the Exodus, yet it was not very long until Israel sinned horribly. Moses confessed: "Oh, this people have sinned a great sin, and have made them gods of gold" (Exodus 32:31). If God were not to forgive the sins of the people of Israel, then Moses' life as liberator of the people and the giver of the law would have been totally wasted. Thus he prayed, "Blot me...out of thy book which thou hast written." That would have been the end of Moses' life in the flesh.

The Book of Life reference is found six times in the

book of Revelation. Verse 5 of chapter 3 reads: "He that overcometh, the same shall be clothed in white raiment; and I will not blot out his name out of the book of life, but I will confess his name before my Father, and before his angels." This is not the eternal Book of Life. This speaks of the life of the Christian who does not overcome, who deliberately sins and does not claim the available power from the Overcomer, who has paid the price for him. Such a Christian would die before his time. His name would be blotted out of the Book of Life, but not of the Book of Life of the Lamb.

Otherwise, this would indicate that a Christian, born again of His Holy Spirit, could lose his salvation. Such teaching contradicts the assurance of salvation God clearly gives in Scripture. Those who deliberately misuse and disregard the cleansing power of the blood of Christ for their own lives will suffer loss, as is recorded in 1 Corinthians 3:15: "If any man's work shall be burned, he shall suffer loss: but he himself shall be saved; yet so as by fire."

"Another Book"

We also see another Book of Life in Revelation 20:12. This is the great white judgment seat, which no longer determines salvation, but condemnation: "And I saw the dead, small and great, stand before God; and the books were opened: and another book was opened, which is the book of life: and the dead were judged out of those things which were written in the books, according to their works." Here an additional Book of Life is revealed. This is the one that documents the life of every person as to his or her deeds.

The absolute separation for all eternity between those whose names were written in the Book of Life but not in the Lamb's Book of Life is documented in Revelation 21:27: "And there shall in no wise enter into it any thing that defileth, neither whatsoever worketh abomination, or maketh a lie: but they which are written in the Lamb's book of life."

I must now ask the question, has your name been added to the Book of Life of the Lamb? Make sure of your answer before the countenance of the Lord, because there is no maybe, could be, or I wish. There is one way or the other. The last verse of John 3 makes this clear: "He that believeth on the Son hath everlasting life: and he that believeth not the Son shall not see life; but the wrath of God abideth on him."

Spiritual Hearing

The next verse is very blunt: "If any man have an ear, let him hear" (Revelation 13:9). Here man is invited to hear if he has an ear. To the Church, the message was similar, yet different. For example, Revelation 2:29: "He that hath an ear, let him hear what the Spirit saith unto the churches." This is the message of the Spirit of God to the churches. But here in Revelation 13:9, the announcement is direct; the Spirit is not mentioned. Why not? Because the Church is no longer on earth; thus "If any man have an ear, let him hear."

What are they supposed to hear? "He that leadeth into captivity shall go into captivity: he that killeth with the sword must be killed with the sword. Here is the patience and the faith of the saints" (verse 10). The last part is the key to understanding this Scripture better: "the patience and the faith of the saints." These saints are admonished to practice patience and faith because the Holy Spirit as the Comforter is no longer on earth.

The Antichrist is praised and worshiped. To the world at large he exhibits himself as the ultimate answer to all the world's ills, but by his actions, he commits blasphemy. Instead of honoring God, he replaces God. He becomes the substitute of God, hence Antichrist. His aim is self-glory.

Self-Glory

We are reminded here of Nebuchadnezzar, the king of the first Gentile superpower. Daniel 4:30 reads: "The king spake, and said, Is not this great Babylon, that I have built for the house of the kingdom by the might of my power, and for the honour of my majesty?" Although King Nebuchadnezzar had experienced the supernatural intervention of the God of Israel on behalf of Daniel on one occasion and

Daniel's three friends on another occasion, he nevertheless exalted himself.

Of King Herod, we read in the New Testament that he did not give God the glory, but accepted the people's judgment that he himself spoke with the voice of God: "And upon a set day Herod, arrayed in royal apparel, sat upon his throne, and made an oration unto them. And the people gave a shout, saying, It is the voice of a god, and not of a man. And immediately the angel of the Lord smote him, because he gave not God the glory: and he was eaten of worms, and gave up the ghost" (Acts 12:21-23). King Herod was another casualty of self-glory.

> *It is important to reemphasize that the Antichrist is an unidentified person who apparently has no power by himself; he is a nobody.*

Antichrist Glory

It is important to reemphasize that the Antichrist is an unidentified person who apparently has no power by himself; he is a nobody. Let's note again that he is the recipient of power from the dragon, "the dragon gave him his power, and his seat, and great authority" (verse 2); "the dragon...gave power unto the beast" (verse 4); "there was given unto him a mouth...and power was given him" (verse 5); "it was given unto him to make war...and power was given unto him" (verse 7). The beast receives supernatural power from the dragon; thus he is able to subdue the whole world under his spell of magic. We must add here that his success is not due to force, but is achieved by deception.

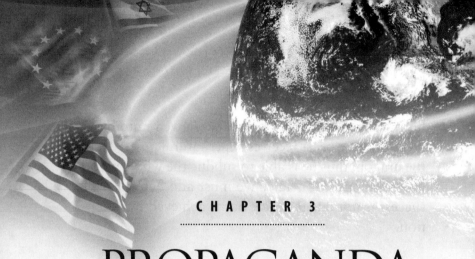

CHAPTER 3

PROPAGANDA MINISTER OF ANTICHRIST

The false prophet uses his power, influence and authority to promote the Antichrist. This is an almost perfect imitation of God the Holy Spirit, who does not glorify Himself, but glorifies Jesus. In this case, the false prophet glorifies Antichrist.

The Second Beast: The False Prophet

"And I beheld another beast coming up out of the earth; and he had two horns like a lamb, and he spake as a dragon" (Revelation 13:11).

We note that the false prophet is coming up out of the earth. That is distinctly different from the first beast, which came up out of the sea. We determined that the sea represents the people of the world—the sea of nations. But the second beast comes out of the earth. That means he is an established identity. His system is already a physical reality on planet Earth. While the first beast received everything from the dragon, the second beast possesses power in his own right—he has power.

Again, we are we reminded of the words of Jesus, "Verily, verily, I say unto you, The Son can do nothing of himself, but what he seeth the Father do: for what things soever he doeth, these also doeth the Son likewise" (John 5:19). Thus we see the first beast, the Antichrist, is the imitation of the Son of God. He has nothing; all things are given to him by the dragon, i.e. Satan. The second beast is the false prophet; we may call him the imitation of the Holy Spirit. His goal is to support, promote, and glorify Antichrist.

The Power of the False Prophet

Verse 11 says, "...he had two horns." What do horns represent in the Bible? Power. But note this power (horns) was not given unto him, but he is the possessor thereof.

What is also striking here is that it says, "two horns like a lamb." We all know that a lamb does not have horns. If it is a male lamb, it will have horns later, but not as a lamb. The lamb is a symbol of meekness, innocence, and has no power in himself. Take note also, it does not say "of a lamb" but "like a lamb." That means this person has the makeup of a religious person, but he is an imitation of the Lamb of God.

Three characteristics are revealed here:

1. The horns represent the political power,
2. The lamb-like figure religious power, and
3. The voice exercises global media power.

We must note again that, contrary to the first beast, to whom "was given…a mouth speaking great things and blasphemies," the second beast has this power on his own authority. He speaks "as a dragon." This is also confirmed in the next verse: "And he exerciseth all the power of the first beast before him, and causeth the earth and them which dwell therein to worship the first beast, whose deadly wound was healed" (Revelation 13:12). In this verse, beast number two is revealed as the propaganda minister of the first beast, the Antichrist.

Diabolical Trinity

The false prophet is a diabolical imitation of the Holy Spirit. When our Lord was on earth, He spoke to His disciples about the coming of the Holy Spirit. Here are His words: "Howbeit when he, the Spirit of truth, is come, he will guide you into all truth: for he shall not speak of himself; but whatsoever he shall hear, that shall he speak: and he will shew you things to come. He shall glorify me: for he shall receive of mine, and shall shew it unto you" (John 16:13-14).

The Holy Spirit guides the Church into all truth. He is not a self-proclaimer, but He shows to the believer the future "things to come." Also, the Holy Spirit "shall glorify me [Jesus]." That is why true Christians do not address the Holy Spirit in their prayer.

Again, we clearly see the imitation of the Holy Trinity. Satan plays the part of God the Father, the Antichrist takes the place of God the Son, and the false prophet takes on the office of the Holy Spirit.

Global Religion

What is the aim of the second beast? For people on earth to worship the first beast. That is global religion. We already saw this in verse 8, where we read, "And all that dwell upon the earth shall worship him." Again, we see that the whole earth is involved. This is Satan's heyday; he has successfully deceived the whole world.

The second beast, the false prophet, uses his power of support to have Antichrist glorified, even worshiped.

Supernatural Events

Scripture identified the Antichrist with a special mark: "whose deadly wound was healed." This wound incident reminds us of the Lord. Thomas, a disciple of Jesus, did not believe: "Except I shall see in his hands the print of the nails and put my finger into the prints of the nails, and thrust my hand into his side, I will not believe" (John 20:25). Jesus revealed Himself to Thomas with these words: "Reach hither thy finger, and behold my hands; and reach hither thy hand, and thrust it into my side: and be not faithless, but believing" (verse 27).

Antichrist is revealed as the one "whose deadly wound was healed." No further information is given in the text as to how this deadly wound was healed, but this seemingly supernatural healing is a power point to magnify Antichrist, elevating him to be a miracle person.

One apparent miracle is followed by another: "And he doeth great wonders, so that he maketh fire come down from heaven on the earth in the sight of men" (verse 13). Here we see the work of a master magician again, the work of Satan.

One thing is clear: This is performed publicly, "in the sight of man." It will be documented by the global media. Books will be written about this amazing man. His message is simple: God has come down to earth, confirmed by supernatural miracles. There is simply no denying of this fact! The time has come to worship this god, visibly demonstrated to all the people of the world.

Not by Force but by Deception

Apparently, there are detractors, those who do not participate or are unsure. Thus he uses an additional method to convince them that the beast is the Christ, the Redeemer of the world: "And deceiveth them that dwell on the earth by the means of those miracles which he had power to do in the sight of the beast; saying to them that dwell on the earth, that they should make an image to the beast, which had the wound by a sword, and did live" (verse 14). Once again, it is needful to point out that the second beast, the false prophet, has power in his possession to do miracles and to command the people that dwell on the earth "that they should make an image to the beast."

Build the Image

The order has gone out to make an image of the Antichrist. But this image, built by man, is unique. It is much more than a picture; it is more than a television or a computer, as we can see from the next verse: "And he had power to give life unto the image of the beast, that the image of the beast should both speak, and cause that as many as would not worship the image of the beast should be killed" (verse 15). Note the words, "he had power" to "give life." Man finally has manufactured an object that has "life."

Artificial Life?

In my library, I have several books and articles written by scholars and brilliant scientists who are convinced that man will be able to create artificial intelligence. One book is titled, *When Things Start to Think* by Neil Gershenfeld.

Can you imagine a man-made product beginning to think?

Another book authored by Robert Buderi carries the title, *Engines of Tomorrow*, subtitled, "How the World's Best Companies Are Using Their Research Labs to Win the Future." Man will create artificial life, but not intelligence. Why not? Because intelligence requires spirit. Man consists of spirit, soul and body, and only God can give spirit.

The Ultimate Authority

Do we have any idea as to the actual makeup of this image? None is given in Scripture; therefore, we should not attempt to let our imaginations run wild. What is clear is that this image not only has life, thus being able to speak, but is capable of distinguishing between those who worship the image of the beast and those who do not. That means this man-made image of the beast has become the ultimate authority over life and death. Those who refuse to worship the image of the beast "should be killed."

Economic Control

Next comes economic and financial control: "And he causeth all, both small and great, rich and poor, free and bond, to receive a mark in their right hand, or in their foreheads: And that no man might buy or sell, save he that had the mark, or the name of the beast, or the number of his name" (verses 16-17).

Again, we may speculate as to the identity of this mark, how it is applied, what it is, how it functions, but we do not find an answer in Scripture. One thing is sure: either you have the mark on the right hand or in the forehead, or you will not be able to buy or sell; subsequently, you will cease to exist.

It would seem obvious that the image of the beast is related to the mark of the beast. Doubtless, this would be accomplished through the most modern communications system planet Earth has ever seen.

The Number 666

Finally, verse 18 says: "Here is wisdom. Let him that hath understanding count the number of the beast: for it is the number of a man; and his number is Six hundred threescore and six." All we know here is that the number of the Antichrist is 666. It is the number of a man. It is the number of the masterpiece of Satan, who presents this man and his image to the nations as Jesus Christ, the Messiah of Israel and the Savior of the world. However, in the end it will be revealed— although too late for those who are deceived—that it was not Jesus, the Son of God who takes away the sins of the world, but an imposter, a wolf in sheep's clothing, a false Jesus, a false prophet, proclaiming a false gospel.

CHAPTER 4

WHEN GOOD IS BAD AND BAD IS GOOD

To better understand the development of prophecy in general, and Revelation 13 in particular, we need to realize that God's thoughts about this world stand diametrically opposed to our thoughts. What we may think is good may be bad in the eyes of God, and what we may think is bad could be good in the eyes of our God.

Worldly Definition

Isaiah 5:20 reads, "Woe unto them that call evil good, and good evil; that put darkness for light, and light for darkness; that put bitter for sweet, and sweet for bitter!"

In order to realize God's intentions with mankind, which He expresses through His prophetic Word, we do well to take careful notice of the above Scripture.

Fundamentally speaking, we have a preconceived definition of good and evil in our minds. Much of this is because we are instructed what is good and evil by our laws. Most laws are based on the fundamentals of the Ten Commandments. This is applicable to all nations of the world, whether communist, democratic, dictatorship, monarchy, or whatever type of government there may be.

We already documented this fact in chapter 1 under the subtitle, "Freedom and God's Grace." When comparing the various major religions and governments, we learn that the fundamental principles of the Ten Commandments are reflected in all global laws. However, keeping the Ten Commandments and being blameless, according to our law or any other law, does not make man good in the eyes of God.

Knowledge of Good and Evil

Another important question that begs an answer is, how do these various nations know what is right and what is wrong? Answer: All nations descend from Adam and Eve, thus all are sinners. Here is what we read in Genesis 3:22: "And the LORD God said, Behold, the man is become as one of us, to know good and evil: and now, lest he put forth his hand, and take also of the tree of life, and eat, and live for ever." Therefore, mankind fundamentally knows what is good and evil because of our original parents, Adam and Eve, who violated God's law by eating of the Tree of Knowledge of Good and Evil. We may say it is in our genes. By nature, man knows the basic fundamentals of good and evil.

When it comes to those who have never heard the Gospel, the Apostle Paul writes in Romans 1:19-20: "Because that which may be known of God is manifest in them; for God hath shewed it unto them. For the invisible things of him from the creation of the world are clearly seen, being understood by the things that are made, even his eternal power and Godhead; so that they are without excuse." Let no one therefore say they are innocent.

> *The fact that we can live in a relatively civilized world under certain laws and order, is not due to our intelligence or to our military strength, but is exclusively and alone due to the grace of God.*

Hell on Earth

The devil, who is the god of this world, is the initiator of evil; he is the murderer from the beginning, the father of lies. But thanks be to God that the devil cannot go beyond the fundamentals of the Ten

Commandments. While he is the prince of darkness who rules planet Earth, he can only act to the limits God has placed on him. If God would withdraw His hand of grace from planet Earth and permit Satan to do as he pleases, then something unspeakably horrendous would happen: the devil would execute his diabolical plan on Earth and we would literally experience hell on earth.

The fact that we can live in a relatively civilized world under certain laws and order, is not due to our intelligence or to our military strength, but is exclusively and alone due to the grace of God. Never give the devil credit for God's work of amazing grace!

What Is Good, What Is Evil?

As law-abiding, hardworking, taxpaying citizens of our respective country, we are considered to be good people. When someone is exceptionally generous, outgoing and friendly, and even sacrifices for the well-being of others, he is rewarded with some kind of honor. That is our definition of good.

The Bible, however, makes a totally different statement. Let's read Isaiah 55:8-9: "For my thoughts are not your thoughts, neither are your ways my ways, saith the LORD. For as the heavens are higher than the earth, so are my ways higher than your ways, and my thoughts than your thoughts." With this statement, we are confronted with an alternative way of measuring. What we call good may not be good, and what we call evil may not be evil in the eyes of the Lord. We need to allow for that possibility, even in our lives.

The Evil World

Take a look at Luke chapter 11. The disciples of Christ asked the Lord to "teach us to pray." He then gives the instruction and says in verse 13: "If ye then, being evil, know how to give good gifts unto your children: how much more shall your heavenly Father give the Holy Spirit to them that ask him?" That is a terrible statement, "ye...being evil"! Jesus calls His very disciples "evil." That is hard to swallow.

Actually, the entire earth is evil, as documented in Galatians 1:4: "Who gave himself for our sins, that he might deliver us from this present evil world, according to the will of God and our Father." This statement teaches us to be very cautious in our definition of good and evil.

Is our country good? Is it really? John puts the world into two categories: "And we know that we are of God, and the whole world lieth in wickedness" (1 John 5:19). Not certain countries, as we like to have it, or as the late President of the United States Ronald Reagan put it, calling the Soviet Union the "Evil Empire." The Bible clearly says, "the whole world lieth in wickedness." We may call ourselves good a million times, but as we have just read, the Bible contradicts us with the thundering statements, "ye...being evil...evil world...whole world lieth in wickedness."

"My Servant" Nebuchadnezzar

King Nebuchadnezzar was the first Gentile super-power ruler. God said: "And now have I given all these lands into the hand of Nebuchadnezzar the king of Babylon, my servant; and the beasts of the field have I given him also to serve him" (Jeremiah 27:6). God calls King Nebuchadnezzar of Babylon "my servant." He, the irresponsible world dictator, who could decide who should live and who should die, is "my servant," says God.

Who would want to live under King Nebuchadnezzar in our days? We read of him in the Book of Daniel and find that his actions were absolutely reckless. He asked his advisers to tell him a dream he had forgotten. Moreover, he expects his advisers to interpret the forgotten dream. Such a request can only be made by a person who is not right in his mind. Yet God calls him "my servant!"

Babylon the Golden

Daniel the prophet comes to the rescue. He tells Nebuchadnezzar precisely what he dreamed, and interprets the dream. Then he makes the following statement: "Thou art this head of gold" (Daniel 2:38). Daniel continues to give a prophetic description of the rest of the world: "And after thee shall arise another kingdom inferior to thee, and another third kingdom of brass, which shall bear rule over all the earth. And the fourth kingdom shall be strong as iron: forasmuch as iron breaketh in pieces and subdueth all things: and as iron that breaketh

81

all these, shall it break in pieces and bruise" (verses 39-40).

We all know that gold is more valuable than silver or brass, and definitely more than iron and clay, of which there is an abundance. But the brutal, oppressive dictator Nebuchadnezzar is declared by God to be leader of the greatest kingdom of the Gentile world—he is the very best. But the last kingdom, which is in our time, the much-praised democratic world, is considered the worst. Do you now see how God calls our good evil and our evil good?

The Last Kingdom: Democracy

Let us take a closer look at Greco-Roman democracy, the political system that is virtually dominating today's world. We cannot deny that democracy has contributed to more freedom for more people in the world than any other system in history. Democracy is the great enemy of dictatorship. In recent years we have seen many dictators fall, and the people of such nations were "liberated" by democracy.

> ✎ The ancient Greek slogan, "Government by the people and for the people" is being practiced globally.

Although the new superpower China is communist, they are operating on a mixture of democratic communism. In the rest of the world, democracy is marching ahead, encompassing planet Earth with the message that people have the right to choose their own government. The ancient Greek slogan, "Government by the people and for the people" is being practiced globally.

When we take time to compare today's democratic governments with Nebuchadnezzar's dictatorship, we most certainly would come to the conclusion that democracy is to be preferred. But God stands in opposition to our conclusion, and He calls the oppressive dictator Nebuchadnezzar good and our so-called democratic freedom evil. He calls Nebuchadnezzar gold and he calls us iron and clay.

Nebuchadnezzar's Quality

Why is Nebuchadnezzar called good and why is democracy called evil? Here is Nebuchadnezzar's own testimony:

> And at the end of the days I Nebuchadnezzar lifted up mine eyes unto heaven, and mine understanding returned unto me, and I blessed the most High, and I praised and honoured him that liveth for ever, whose dominion is an everlasting dominion, and his kingdom is from generation to generation: And all the inhabitants of the earth are reputed as nothing: and he doeth according to his will in the army of heaven, and among the inhabitants of the earth: and none can stay his hand, or say unto him, What doest thou? At the same time my reason returned unto me; and for the glory of my kingdom, mine honour and brightness returned unto me; and my counsellors and my lords sought unto me; and I was established in my kingdom, and excellent majesty was added unto me. Now I Nebuchadnezzar praise and extol and honour the King of heaven, all whose works are truth, and his ways judgment: and those that walk in pride he is able to abase (Daniel 4:34-37).

Nebuchadnezzar personally recognized the God of Heaven and gave honor to Him.

Democracy Versus God

In today's democratic world, God is either outright rejected in the process of government or is used as a band-aid for the benefit of modern democratic society. Or, as Oswald Chambers said, "...Our god is the conventional righteousness of the society to which we belong" (*Daily Thoughts For Disciples*, 28 March, Barbour Publishing, 1976).

What happened in the beginning, listed in the sixth chapter of Genesis, is applicable for today as well: "And GOD saw that the wickedness of man was great in the earth, and that every imagination of the thoughts of his heart was only evil continually" (Genesis 6:5). It stands to reason that if man, whose heart is evil continually, were to rule himself, only evil can be the ultimate result. The Bible delivers a devastating blow to humanity by declaring unilaterally that all people, all nations on planet Earth are fundamentally evil.

Democracy, on the other hand, desperately attempts to show the good side of man, believing that humanity can produce a peaceful, prosperous, and secure global society without Jesus Christ the Crucified.

Good or Evil?

While writing these lines, I fully realize that such statements are difficult to accept, but I am convinced that this is what Scripture teaches, and is how God sees us. It is for this reason the overwhelming majority of the intellectuals of this world outright reject the Gospel of Jesus Christ as the only remedy for man's sin. Thus, we read Paul's declaration: "For the preaching of the cross is to them that perish foolishness; but unto us which are saved it is the power of God" (1 Corinthians 1:18).

Are you beginning to see that that which we have determined to be good, God calls evil, and that which we have determined to be evil, God calls good?

Hope for the Hopeless

When we understand these fundamentals, our spiritual eyes and ears will be open to the wonderful message God intends to give His people.

God's judgment is very plain: He declares that you and I are evil, the whole world is evil, and that there is no good in man whatsoever. Man is corrupt through and through, and is on his way to eternal damnation. When we grasp this truth, we realize with horror that our position really is hopeless.

But thank God, there is an escape. Hebrews 9:14 reads: "How much more shall the blood of Christ, who through the eternal Spirit offered himself without spot to God, purge your conscience from dead works to serve the living God?"

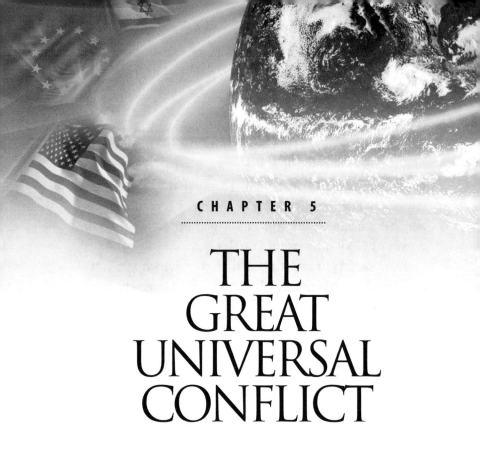

CHAPTER 5

THE GREAT UNIVERSAL CONFLICT

The world's most successful political philosophy—democracy—when analyzed in light of Holy Scripture, contains a fatal flaw: People rule people. The strength of democracy lies in numbers. When numbers become the majority, then the majority becomes the ultimate authority for rules of life, justice, morals, laws, and educational institutions. Furthermore, global democracy will lead to the ultimate battle, but is it physical or spiritual?

The False Messiah

"And I saw one of his heads as it were wounded to death; and his deadly wound was healed: and all the world wondered after the beast" (Revelation 13:3).

Once again, we want to emphasize the words, "all the world." The whole world is admiring, is astonished and amazed at the miraculous healing of the deadly wound.

It is needful to mention that this is not speaking of a real monster having seven heads and ten horns. This beast is the Antichrist, who is a person possessed by the devil. The purpose of his existence is to present himself to the world as God:

> *Therefore to picture in one's mind an unknown animal, a seven-headed monster will lead us astray from the message of Holy Scripture.*

"...so that he as God sitteth in the temple of God, shewing himself that he is God" (2 Thessalonians 2:4). This is the false Messiah, the one Jesus prophesied about when He said, "I am come in my Father's name, and ye receive me not: if another shall come in his own name, him ye will receive" (John 5:43). Therefore to picture in one's mind an unknown animal, a seven-headed monster will lead us astray from the message of Holy Scripture.

Things Out of This World

John is in heaven and sees something that is totally out of this world, but he must describe this for us in earthly terms. Note also that it says, "as it were wounded to death." In plain words, it's not a "dead head." It only seemed as if it were dead. In verse 2 we read the description of the beast, which says, "the beast which I saw was like unto…." The beast was not a leopard, a bear or a lion, but a very distinct personality with the characteristics of these animals.

I think we would agree that it is virtually impossible to transfer this vision in earthly pictures. All we can come up with is an artist's conception of a horrible monster with seven heads. Such a picture, however, would definitely lead us in the wrong direction in our study. Why? Because this beast represents the whole world. All have become one in their praise, admiration, and even worship of this beast.

Rome Healed by Religion

How is it possible for a diverse world to be so united? For one thing, they are convinced by an undeniable miracle: "his deadly wound was healed."

Now we may ask a question: Is this future or has the healing of the "deadly wound" already occurred? We know that the beast embodies the political, economic and religious capacity of the entire world. This is the last power structure in the line of Gentile superpowers. It is the iron-clay kingdom, which is the Roman world empire, according to the prophet Daniel.

History clearly teaches that Rome did receive a deadly wound when the northern European barbarians destroyed Rome. It should have been the end of the Roman Empire, but lo and behold, the embodiment of Rome still lives today. Why? Because the political power structure of the Roman Empire was transferred to

> *The political power structure of the Roman Empire was transferred to the religious power structure, administered by the new religious culture, headed by one man, the Pope of Rome.*

the religious power structure, administered by the new religious culture, headed by one man, the Pope of Rome. This religious structure has claimed civil power, not only over Rome, but also over the entire world.

E-Sword quotes *Barnes Commentary:*

> And his deadly wound was healed—the waning Roman secular power was restored by its connection with the spiritual power—the papacy. This was:
>
> (a)A simple matter of fact, that the waning secular power of Rome was thus restored by connecting itself with the spiritual or ecclesiastical power, thus prolonging what might properly be called the Roman domination far beyond what it would otherwise have been; and,
>
> (b)This would be properly represented by just the symbol employed here—the fatal wound inflicted on the head, and the healing of that wound, or preventing what would naturally be the effects.

We must therefore come to the conclusion that the deadly wound was healed and continues to be healed until this very day.

Now a question: Will Rome be the capital of the New World Order?

First, we must understand that Rome plays a much greater role than just being the capital city of Italy. The Roman system dominates four of the world's five continents. Europe, Africa, America and Australia can be considered as predominantly European. The languages are European and their constitutions, systems of law and business practices are all based on Roman laws.

But the Asian continent also depends upon European philosophies and laws. Asian nations are likely to use a European language to communicate with each other. The implementation of laws and conducting of businesses are firmly grounded on Roman principles as well.

Ancient Rome brought the highest glory to Europe. And Europe is the only continent that has permanently molded the nations of the world. The Africans did not establish colonies in America, nor did the Asians do so in Africa, but the Europeans, which we can rightfully call Romans, colonialized almost the entire world. *(119 Most Frequently Asked Questions About Prophecy,* 100).

6,000 Years of Counterfeit Redemption

Often we seem to confuse God's plan of salvation with certain fulfillment of Bible prophecy, without realizing that approximately 6,000 years are involved in the process. When man fell into sin, God had a plan to redeem man. We all know the promise of the Savior found in Genesis 3:15: "And I will put enmity between thee and the woman, and between thy seed and her seed; it shall bruise thy head, and thou shalt bruise his heel." Quite naturally, parallel to God's plan of salvation, Satan has a plan of destruction, and he accomplishes it through deception. Thus we must learn to distinguish between the real and the fake; between God's plan of salvation, which leads to eternal joy, and Satan's counterfeit plan of salvation, which ends in eternal damnation. But all this has been ongoing for about 6,000 years.

Before the Foundation of the World

When we place fulfillment of Bible prophecy within the timeframe of the Great Tribulation, for example, we are really missing the point. Prophecy must be understood from eternal perspectives. We must not attempt to force it into a straightjacket of the seven-year tribulation or the 2,000 years during the Church age. Note carefully the words of 1 Peter 1:20: "Who verily was foreordained before the foundation of the world, but was manifest in these last times for you." Also, we have read Revelation 13:8 several times, where it states: "the Lamb slain from the foundation of the world."

> *Satan has a plan of destruction, and he accomplishes it through deception.*

It is helpful to realize that when we speak about God, we are speaking of eternity. That means no beginning and no end. Nevertheless, in the fullness of time, God did contact planet Earth, when He sent His Son to accomplish redemption. And when the time comes, the Son will come back in the clouds of heaven, but the year, day or hour of His return is hidden from us. Any speculation will only lead us astray.

The Times of the Gentiles

Let's see an example in Daniel 2:44: "And in the days of these kings shall the God of heaven set up a kingdom, which shall never be destroyed: and the kingdom shall not be left to other people, but it shall break in pieces and consume all these kingdoms, and it shall stand for ever."

> *God is setting up His Kingdom, although we perceive no visible manifestation of this work on earth now.*

Note, this speaks of the four kings and kingdoms: Babylon, Persia, Greece and Rome. God's Word tells us, "In the days of these kings shall the God of heaven set up a kingdom, which shall never be destroyed." "These days" are about 2,600 years long! That simply means that during these 2,600 years, the times of the Gentiles, God is setting up His Kingdom, although we perceive no visible manifestation of this work on earth now.

We must learn to see Scripture from God's perspective. His thoughts are much higher than ours. Only through the Holy Spirit can we grasp the full truth that is being conveyed to us in Holy Scripture. Otherwise, it just become words, definitions and descriptions of some unknown "out of this world" objects or events.

Preparation Time

Revelation 13 speaks of the past, the present and the future. But, it is important to emphasize the climaxing fulfillment of prophecy in our days. How is it possible for the diverse world to become one? That is the subject we want to discuss further.

Let us now take a closer look at how this event of political globalism is developing:

> And the sixth angel poured out his vial upon the great river Euphrates; and the water thereof was dried up, that the way of the kings of the east might be prepared. And I saw three unclean spirits like frogs come out of the mouth of the dragon, and out of the mouth of the beast, and out of the mouth of the false prophet. For they are the spirits of devils, working miracles, which go forth unto the kings of the earth and of the whole world, to gather them to the battle of that great day of God Almighty (Revelation 16:12-14).

What we have just read can be titled "progressive fulfillment of prophecy." These few words describe the end stages of the end times. It will climax in the confrontation between the powers of darkness and the Lord God

93

Almighty. But keep in mind that this has been in preparation for roughly 6,000 years.

We may call this the end result of Satan's master plan for humanity. He is the father of lies, the author of confusion, and the master of deception. Just as he was successful in deceiving Eve to take the fruit of the tree of knowledge of good and evil, Satan continues to be very successful in his cunning ways with all of humanity until this very day.

> *This is a spiritual battle, but the physical world is involved.*

Physical or Spiritual?

When reading these verses (Revelation 16:12-14), we immediately are confronted with the question, "Is this to be taken literally, or is it spiritual?" The answer is both. Let's look at some facts. We do have geographic references such as the Euphrates River. It actually says, "The water thereof was dried up." This can hardly be spiritualized. Further, in verse 14 it speaks of "the kings of the earth and of the whole world." Kings represent the world's political leaders. Note the words "whole world." This really speaks of global physical substance.

But that is one side of the story. Because the initiating activity is accomplished by a heavenly identity—"the sixth angel poured out his vial"—this action results in the revelation of three unclean spirits. They proceed from the dragon, the beast and the false prophet. They are the devil, the Antichrist and the false prophet. Here the connection between the visible and the invisible world is revealed. Such is also the case in verse 14, where we read of "spirits" and of "the kings of the earth." Thus, we are dealing with spiritual and physical entities.

> ✎ *It is the Lord Himself who gathers together the rebellious world in order to execute judgment.*

A Different Battle

What is the purpose of this global deception? "...To gather them to the battle of that great day of God Almighty." We know that it is impossible for man to make war against God. Man's weapons—planes, tanks, bombs and bullets—need an earthly physical target. In other words, an enemy has to be identified in order to be attacked. But how is anyone going to identify God Almighty physically? That is impossible; thus, weapons of war as we know them are out of contention. This is a spiritual battle, but the physical world is involved.

Later in Revelation 19 we read of the intent of Satan and his Antichrist:

> And I saw the beast, and the kings of the earth, and their armies, gathered together to make war against him that sat on the horse, and against his army. And the beast was taken, and with him the false prophet that wrought miracles before him, with which he deceived them that had received the mark of the

95

beast, and them that worshipped his image. These both were cast
alive into a lake of fire burning with brimstone (verses 19-20).

The purpose of the gathering of the armed forces of the
world is to fight against the Anointed; that is, the Lord
Himself. In reality, however, it is the Lord who gathers
together the rebellious world in order to execute judgment.

A No-Weapon War

Again, will this be a literal, physical war? Most scholars and commentaries indicate a physical war to take
place; I venture to say no. Why not? Because the Lord is
the undisputed Victor: He does not need to fight. He is the
sovereign Judge of heaven and earth. He only needs to
appear and speak, to expose and destroy the powers of
Satan and his servants.

This is documented, for example, in 2 Thessalonians
2:8: "And then shall that Wicked be revealed, whom the
Lord shall consume with the spirit of his mouth, and shall
destroy with the brightness of his coming." Here we see
the weapons of warfare, "the spirit of His mouth" and
"the brightness of His coming." That is the epitome of the
Battle of Armageddon, the annihilation of Satan's masterpiece, the Antichrist.

A Non-Earthly Physical War

This non-physical warfare is also revealed in the text
we just read, "And the beast was taken, and with him the

false prophet…" (Revelation 19:20). There is no record of any contention between the Lord and the beast or the false prophet. They are simply arrested. They do not appear before the final judgment seat of God, but they are directly and immediately condemned, and judgment is executed: "[They] were cast alive into a lake of fire burning with brimstone." There is no physical, military battle recorded for us. Jesus is Victor: He need not fight for victory.

The Army Without Weapons

Let us again read Revelation 19:19: "And I saw the beast, and the kings of the earth, and their armies, gathered together to make war against him that sat on the horse, and against his army." Here we

> *He only needs to appear and speak, to expose and destroy the powers of Satan and his servants.*

have two armies: one is under the authority of the beast, and the other is of the Lord, the "King of kings and Lord of lords." We all know who it is "that sat on the horse." He is the one revealed in the previous verses: "And I saw heaven opened, and behold a white horse; and he that sat upon him was called Faithful and True, and in righteousness he doth judge and make war" (verse 11). We need to be careful not to mix the earthly physical with the heavenly physical. When it says "white horse" and "make war," it is to be understood as "heavenly physical."

The description of His army is given in verse 14: "And the armies which were in heaven followed him upon white horses, clothed in fine linen, white and clean." This Army is not an army as we understand it from earthly perspectives. They have no weapons! They belong to Him who is the Word of God.

An Out of This World War

How does the war proceed? Let's read verse 15: "And out of his mouth goeth a sharp sword, that with it he should smite the nations: and he shall rule them with a rod of iron: and he treadeth the winepress of the fierceness and wrath of Almighty God." There is no comparison of such an event on earth; this is clearly "out of this world."

> *The whole world, under the authority of the beast, gathers with the intention to make war, but nothing is going to materialize except their own destruction.*

I venture to say that the assumption Jesus comes with His saints all riding on white horses to the earth, to fight against the nations of the world, is not really supported by Scripture. Jesus does not need to war against the beast, nor against the nations, but as we have already read, "the Lord shall consume [the Antichrist] with the Spirit of his mouth, and shall destroy with the brightness of his coming" (2 Thessalonians 2:8). That's a different story all together. When He appears in the brightness of His coming, truth will be made a visible reality and deception and lies will be exposed. Please keep in mind that light is stronger than darkness. The whole world,

> Pride is a trademark of the devil and should have no room in the life of a Christian.

under the authority of the beast, gathers with the intention to make war, but nothing is going to materialize except their own destruction.

The Whole World

It is important to reemphasize that this is globalism. The entire world is involved; no nation is exempt. When it says, "the kings of the earth and of the whole world," it is clear that all of humanity has become subject to the authority of the god of this world, who is revealed with a fourfold title in Revelation 12:9: "dragon...old serpent...Devil...and Satan."

Nationalism

Whenever I speak or write about the world and the evil therein, there are a number of well-meaning Christians who try desperately to exclude their own nation from the evil world. This is due to the spirit of national pride. Pride is a trademark of the devil and should have no room in the life of a Christian. The Bible clearly says, "the whole world lieth in wickedness" (1 John 5:19). It does not matter whether we call ourselves a peace-loving nation, whether Christian, Muslim, Hindu, Buddhist, atheist, agnostic, communist, socialist, capitalist or monarchist. Nothing changes the Scripture's declaration: "the whole world lieth in wickedness." That should not be difficult to understand, unless you have been deceived and national pride has robbed you of your ability to understand Bible truth.

The Wrong Enemies

We tend to follow in the footsteps of the world's media, which always tries to identify some other evil in the world, but never our own. From the early 1960s until the 80s, it was communism. An immense volume of propaganda was produced, not only by the so-called Western world, but also by Churchianity as well, always identifying communism as the evil and the hindering element for world peace.

Since 9/11, the Arab-Muslim nations are the target of Christian propaganda, which identifies them as the real problem in this world and the hindrance to global peace. Yet the Bible says, "the whole world lieth in wickedness." It does not matter what political persuasion or religion we may adhere to: the Bible devastates all the theories with the words, "He that committeth sin is of the devil" (1 John 3:8). Anyone here without sin?

One Exception

There is one exception, and that is God's new creature: "Whosoever is born of God doth not commit sin; for his seed remaineth in him: and he cannot sin, because he is born of God" (1 John 3:9). That speaks of God's new creation through Jesus Christ. He who is born again of the Spirit of God "cannot sin." This must not be misunderstood. That which is born again still resides in the perishable tabernacle of flesh and blood, and is capable of the worst sin anyone can commit. We must never think that Christians cannot sin—that is far from the truth. Only that which is born of God is perfect, sinless and eternal.

> *Only that which is born of God is perfect, sinless and eternal.*

I am aware that some teach earthly perfection, but that would mean a Christian would live sinless in his flesh. Let us read the last five verses of 1 John chapter 1, and note the word "if":

> If we say that we have fellowship with him, and walk in darkness, we lie, and do not the truth: But if we walk in the light, as he is in the light, we have fellowship one with another, and the blood of Jesus Christ his Son cleanseth us from all sin. If we say that we have no sin, we deceive ourselves, and the truth is not in us. If we confess our sins, he is faithful and just to forgive us our sins, and to cleanse us from all unrighteousness. If we say that we have not sinned, we make him a liar, and his word is not in us (1 John 1:6-10).

The last verse in particular reveals the impossibility of perfection in the flesh.

Political Globalism

The three parts of this book identify globalism in its various forms. In our days, it is an undeniable fact: Globalism affects every person on planet Earth. But globalism is not something new; it is actually very old. We find the record in Genesis 11. Here we read of man's attempt to establish political globalism. The time was, according to the margin of my Bible, 1491 B.C. Here is the story:

> *A stone is very unique: there are no two stones alike on planet Earth.*

And the whole earth was of one language, and of one speech. And it came to pass, as they journeyed from the east, that they found a plain in the land of Shinar; and they dwelt there. And they said one to another, Go to, let us make brick, and burn them throughly. And they had brick for stone, and slime had they for morter. And they said, Go to, let us build us a city and a tower, whose top may reach unto heaven; and let us make us a name, lest we be scattered abroad upon the face of the whole earth (Genesis 11:1-4).

We note, "The whole earth was of one language." Globalism was a reality at that time, because man could

102

communicate with one another. That seems to be good. However, there is an arrogance expressed in the words "us" and "we." They begin with a political philosophy (democracy), followed by materialism (capitalism), and aimed to reach heaven—that is religious globalism.

The Power of Uniformity

There is a prophetic picture in the use of the building material. Instead of stone, the natural material, they fabricated bricks. A stone is very unique: there are no two stones alike on planet Earth. You

> Equality is the driving force to unify the world.

can compare billions, even trillions, of stones, yet they are all different. But bricks can be made into a nearly perfect identical form—all can become alike. This is a prophetic picture of our world today. Equality is the driving force to unify the world.

The distinct difference between male and female as documented in Scripture, has virtually ceased to exist, even in our churches. The political system of democracy has put on even keel the rich and the poor, the wise and the simple, the good and the bad. It is not surprising that marriage is now being challenged. Sodomites want to be treated equally. In the building of the Tower of Babel, we see these bricks representing the equality of all humans on planet Earth.

Furthermore, they had "slime for mortar." This is quite

interesting, because mortar is usually a weaker substance when used to assemble stones or bricks. Although mortar holds them together, the stones or bricks can be separated relatively easy. But the use of "slime," better translated as tar oil or bitumen, is the substance used to glue those "bricks" together, making the structure virtually impossible to disassemble. The global union that is now being formed is glued together inseparably. What is this "slime" of today? Isn't it oil? The oil from below is the adhesive that holds the industrialized nations of the world together. In contrast, the oil from above, the Holy Spirit, holds the Church together.

Babylon's Reach Unto Heaven

The people of Babel continue building a mighty city with a tower *"whose top may reach unto heaven."* It seems reasonable to assume that these people were intelligent enough to know that heaven could not be reached. What becomes evident is that they wanted to reach heaven on their own terms. But man can never reach God. So what did God do in the fullness of time? He reached down to earth. God came to earth in the flesh and dwelt among us. He became man, and thereby created the only way to escape the cursed earth. How? By dying. That is the message of the New Testament: through death to glory. It means the old nature, our flesh and blood, our self, has to identify with the death of the cross. That's the only way to heaven. Romans 6:5 says: "For if we have been planted together in the likeness of his death, we shall be also in the likeness of his resurrection."

Also, the citizens of Babel expressed their rebellion against the God of heaven, who instructed Adam and Eve to "replenish the earth." They had no intention of being scattered abroad upon the face of the whole earth. They wanted to build their Babylon, their own pride, their own way to heaven.

The driving motive of these people was pride, "Let us make us a name." Until this very day, nations all over the world are trying to accomplish greater things, building larger and taller buildings to demonstrate their pride over other nations.

Language Confusion

How does God answer? "And the LORD said, Behold, the people is one, and they have all one language; and this they begin to do: and now nothing will be restrained from them, which they have imagined to do" (Genesis 11:6).

> ✎ *The oil from below is the adhesive that holds the industrialized nations of the world together. In contrast, the oil from above, the Holy Spirit, holds the Church together.*

This verse reconfirms globalism, particularly with the words, "nothing will be restrained from them [the whole world], which they have imagined to do."

What did God do? "Go to, let us go down, and there

confound their language, that they may not understand one another's speech. So the LORD scattered them abroad from thence upon the face of all the earth: and they left off to build the city" (verses 7-8). From that point on man was separated by languages; one could not understand the other. What did men do? They used their swords (weapons of war) to communicate with one another. From that time on innumerable wars have been fought throughout the world. Even today there are conflicts which man tries to solve with weapons of war.

Why Different Languages?

There is a question that may come to our mind: Why doesn't God permit a one-language world? The Europeans created a universal language called Esperanto. It was developed in the late 1870s by Dr. Ludwig Lazarus Zamenhof, a Jewish ophthalmologist from Poland. But, according to Wikepedia, this language is spoken fluently by less than 2 million people. That fact shows that Esperanto was and is a failure.

English has developed to be the most prominent European language and is often called the world language. But those who travel often know that outside airports, tourist attractions and the upper echelon in the business world, everyone continues to communicate in their own language. If you do not speak Portuguese, for example, you will not get very far in Brazil. Even in countries whose official second language is English, you will not be able to communicate with the people on the street unless you speak their language.

We must come to the conclusion, therefore, that God had a very specific reason in confusing the languages. What is that reason? When the nations fight against each other, they will not unite against God. Today, however,

> ✍ *When the nations fight against each other, they will not unite against God.*

man is detouring the language barriers with his own inventions: communication by wire, airwaves and satellites, and instant translation. Globalism on all levels has become a household word, and in the end, as we have already read in Revelation 16 and 17, man will unite for one purpose alone: opposing Almighty God.

Satan's intention is increasingly being revealed in these days. He strives for world unity, and based on the prophetic Word, he will be successful. Why does the world follow him? Because they have chosen not to believe in Jesus: "In whom the god of this world hath blinded the minds of them which believe not, lest the light of the glorious gospel of Christ, who is the image of God, should shine unto them" (2 Corinthians 4:4).

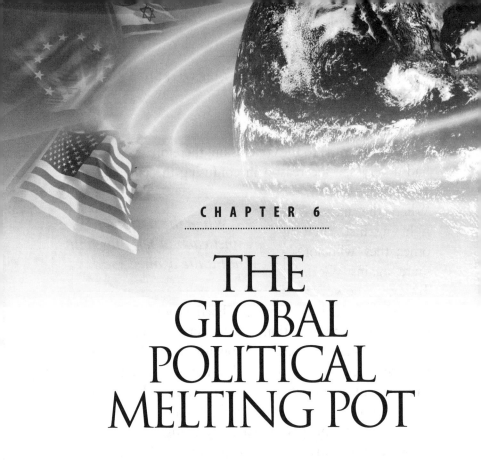

CHAPTER 6

THE GLOBAL POLITICAL MELTING POT

True global unity requires cooperation between the nations of the world. Democracy is one of the major tools by which unity can be achieved. In this chapter, we will see how the various political movements adopt a mixture of capitalism, socialism and communism to attain their goal. What seemed impossible just a few decades ago is now practiced in reality. For example, democratic America is utilizing communist principles to save their financial infrastructure, while communist China is making use of democratic principles. Where will it all lead? To the fulfillment of Revelation 17:13:"These have one mind, and shall give their power and strength unto the beast."

Communism, Socialism and Capitalism United

On the way to a truly global planet, there is one issue the world has to face: China is a communist country and a candidate for becoming the leading nation in the world. This nation has been able to turn the tables; they no longer are depending on capitalist help. China holds more than a trillion dollars in cash and government bonds in support of the United States. One does not need a Ph.D. in finances to realize that communist China could apply a devastating blow to the United States if they were to sell their American assets. This would cause the U.S. dollar to become relatively valueless.

But there is a problem: China can't do it because the United States is the second largest customer of China's gigantic manufacturing industry. Thus, commerce has locked these two opposing factions into a virtually inseparable unity.

China Says Oust Dollar as International Reserve Currency

China's central bank proposed replacing the US dollar as the international reserve currency with a new global system controlled by the International Monetary Fund.

In an essay posted on the People's Bank of China's website, Zhou Xiaochuan, the central bank's governor, said the goal would be to create a reserve currency "that is disconnected from individual nations and is able to remain stable in the long run, thus removing the inherent deficiencies caused by using credit-based national currencies."

Analysts said the proposal was an indication of Beijing's fears that actions being taken to save the domestic US economy would have a negative impact on China.

"This is a clear sign that China, as the largest holder of US dollar financial assets, is concerned about the potential inflationary risk of the US Federal Reserve printing money," said Qu Hongbin, chief China economist for HSBC.

China has little choice but to hold the bulk of its $2,000bn of foreign exchange reserves in US dollars, and this is unlikely to change in the near future.

To replace the current system, Mr Zhou suggested expanding the role of special drawing rights, which were introduced by the IMF in 1969 to support the Bretton Woods fixed exchange rate regime but became less relevant once that collapsed in the 1970s.

China's proposal would expand the basket of currencies forming the basis of SDR valuation to all major economies and set up a settlement system between SDRs and other currencies so they could be used in international trade and financial transactions.

Countries would entrust a portion of their SDR reserves to the IMF to manage collectively on their behalf and SDRs would gradually replace existing reserve currencies.

Mr Zhou said the proposal would require "extraordinary political vision and courage" and acknowledged a debt to John Maynard Keynes, who made a similar suggestion in the 1940s.

-Financial Times, 24 March 2009, pg. 1

How irreversibly China and the U.S.A. are linked together, was highlighted in an article by the *EU Observer*, 2 February 2009: "China and the U.S. must operate together because their economies have become inseparable twins."

Communist Banks of America

What was unthinkable only a few decades ago is happening today. China is applying capitalist principles, while the United States is becoming deeply entrenched in social communist principles. This was vividly demonstrated when the U.S. government was forced to bail out banks and financial institutions. A foundational communist principle is that the government owns and controls part or all of financial institutions.

Even Europe, the world's socialist powerhouse, refused to apply American financial socialism during the recent financial fiasco.

Often the question is asked: Will China becomes a democratic nation? That is very difficult to visualize, since they have become extremely successful under their own much praised and celebrated communist system. What is the answer then? Based on our understanding of prophetic Scripture, each nation in the world may continue to function in their own political and economic system, applying their own national laws and regulations, but under the umbrella of a New World Order. China does not need to convert to democratic capitalism. They may continue with their communist system, which apparently serves them rather well. China is becoming a power structure of great significance. In January of 2009, China replaced Germany as the world's third largest economy. Based on the predictions of global economists, Germany, the world's largest exporter, will lose its position to China within a few years.

The *New* New World Order

A review of recent history gives us a better picture of the development toward a one world. When Soviet communism defeated Nazism, it was assumed that communism would sweep over all of Europe and virtually dominate the rest of the world. That, as we all know, did not materialize.

Capitalism, American brand, was expected by many to sweep the planet, but that, too, did not take place.

Then something new happened. The date was 25 March 1957. The Treaty of Rome was signed, establishing the European Economic Community (EEC). The first order of business was abolishing customs duties between the countries of Germany, France, Italy, Luxembourg, Belgium, and the Netherlands. This was the beginning of the *new* New World Order. These six nations—diverse in language, culture, customs and history—created a new economic reality, which surpassed their diversity in an unprecedented way. Something had been created that allowed the individual member nation to retain its identity, but pledge economic unity under the umbrella of the EEC.

The European Model

The European Union has established the workable model for the world. Today, at the time of writing, twenty-seven nations are united as members of the Union, although each continues to function within its own sovereignty. Each has its own unique history, language, culture, tradition, customs and national holidays, yet they have become united under the umbrella of the European Union.

The following is a summary from a book entitled, *The European Dream: How Europe's Vision of the Future is Quietly Eclipsing the American Dream,* by Jeremy Rifkin, Published by Tarchev in 2004.

The European Dream should be required reading on both sides of the Atlantic. To Americans it sounds the alarm. At the height of the supposed unipolar dominance of the US, fewer and fewer foreigners view it as an attractive model for constitutions, companies or communities. To Europeans, Rifkin issues the challenge of global leadership.

Europe is really "best positioned between the extreme individualism of America and the extreme collectivism of Asia to lead the way into the new age."

Inflows of foreign nationals, standardised data
As a percentage of the total population, 2004

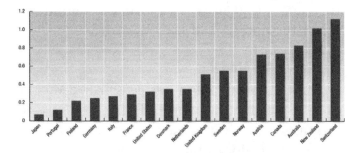

Source: OECD Factbook 2007 –
Economic, Environmental and Social Statistics

The Melting of Political Philosophies

When analyzing the events taking place today, many seem to overlook the fact that the major political and economic philosophies—democracy, communism, socialism, dictatorship, monarchy—have already merged to such an extent that it would be impossible to separate them.

Although in the United States, the terms communist and socialist are vehemently opposed and outright rejected, a closer look reveals that the functionality of the government, the economy and particularly the financial institutions is already grounded solidly on the pillars of communism and socialism—yet most of us are still in denial.

Socialism at Work

During the recent financial chaos we saw the government becoming part owners of banks, financial institutions and insurance, which is a trademark of communist socialism. Whenever the government pays for a project, it is said to be using "taxpayer money." But what is "taxpayer money?" It is nothing other than the social product of the nation. Governments collect taxes and spend it, preferably for the well-being of their citizens. That's 100 percent socialism.

When we honestly analyze our system here in the U.S., we must come to the conclusion that there is no such thing as true capitalism. At most, there is a degree of capitalism that plays a role within our nation, but pure capitalism ceased to exist long ago. We may hate to admit it or deny it as much as we want, but that does not change the fact that socialism is the driving force of the so-called capitalist world.

> *Democracy, communism, socialism, dictatorship, monarchy—have already merged to such an extent that it would be impossible to separate them.*

Let's look at a few items. Take our armed forces: they are greatly honored and respected in this country. Who is paying the bill? Answer: socialism (social capital). That is the only product the government produces. You are duty bound, required by law to pay your taxes to the Internal Revenue Service for the collective well-being of the nation—that is socialism.

Take a closer look at our communication and transportation systems, particularly the interstate system. Who paid for it? Answer: socialism (social capital). Remember that the next time you drive your car on a public road.

How did America get a man to the moon? Who paid for it? Again, the answer is socialism (social-capital).

Agricultural Socialism

One of the most obvious socialist successes is our much-praised "capitalist" agriculture industry. But lo and behold, again we find tax money (social capital) at work.

> *The USDA subsidies for farms in the state of South Carolina totaled $1,052,000,000 between 1995–2006.*

Here in our state, South Carolina, the federal government supports the agriculture industry, including tobacco growers, to the tune of hundreds of millions of dollars. The USDA subsidies for farms in the state of South Carolina totaled $1,052,000,000 between 1995–2006 (Source: Environmental Working Group's Subsidy Database, farm.ewg.org).

One would think that the fundamentals of capitalism are manifested best by farmers who own the land, pro-

THE GLOBAL POLITICAL MELTING POT

duce food and sell it for profit. Not so. Tax-based socialism is the key to this success. This system is not only practiced in the U.S.A., but more so in Europe. These few examples should suffice to show that capitalism, socialism and communism have united. Capital socialism is the bedrock foundation of the United States of America.

We often assume that foreign countries violate international law when it comes to subsidies, but as the following article reveals, subsidies, legal or illegal, are a two-way street.

Brazil to Dispute US Subsidies

Brazil is preparing to take action against the US over what it says are illegal subsidies and other trade barriers following the collapse of the Doha round of talks at the World Trade Organization in Geneva.

"The clock is ticking," Celso Amorim, Brazil's foreign minister, told the Financial Times in his first interview after returning from the failed talks. "Our understanding with the US was good throughout and it never came to acrimony. But they are the biggest subsidizers in the world in terms of what affects us, so we will have to see them in court."

The WTO upheld a complaint by Brazil that Washington had not done enough to remove illegal subsidies to its cotton farmers, opening the way for Brazil to request WTO authorization for more than $1bn in retaliatory sanctions on US services and intellectual property.

Mr Amorim said Brazil would still rather avoid taking

action but that this was now the only option.

In addition to retaliatory measures on US cotton subsidies, Brazil would prepare legal action against US import tariffs on Brazilian ethanol of 54 cents a gallon, which Mr Amorim described as "discriminatory."

Brazil's agricultural sector has expanded strongly in recent years, and the country has become the world's biggest producer and exporter of several foods as well as industrial commodities. It had much to gain from the Doha conference and played a leading role in the talks, making a series of concessions in the hope of achieving a multilateral agreement.

-Financial Times, 4 August 2008, pg. 2

Here is my commentary:

To most Americans, this sounds unusual and strange. After all, the U.S.A. prides itself on being a non-socialist, capitalist nation. But, as evidenced by this and many other reports, there is no longer such a thing as capitalism. The global world has developed into a mixture of capital/social communism. That is to be expected, particularly with the bailout of financial institutions and banks. The U.S. has joined the international family of functional socialism.

From prophetic perspectives, we have to realize that only one system can bring forth the required unity for the new global world order, and that is a mixture of capitalism, socialism and communism *(Midnight Call,* January 2009).

Is World Government Possible?

We have already read of the success of this super man we call the Antichrist: "And all the world wondered after the beast" (verse 3). But there are many seemingly insurmountable problems toward achieving this global unity. Yet, we can be sure of one thing: it will happen. World government will be implemented.

An article in the *Financial Times*, 9 December 2008, pg. 13, argues the possibility:

> A 'world government' would involve much more than co-operation between nations. It would be an entity with state-like characteristics, backed by a body of laws. The European Union has already set up a continental government for 27 countries, which could be a model. The EU has a supreme court, a currency, thousands of pages of law, a large civil service and the ability to deploy military force.
>
> So could the European model go global? There are three reasons for thinking that it might.
>
> First, it is increasingly clear that the most difficult issues facing national governments are international in nature: there is global warming, a global financial crisis and a 'global war on terror.'
>
> Second, it could be done. The transport and communications revolutions have shrunk the world so that, as Geoffrey Blainey, an eminent Australian historian, has written: 'For the first time in human history, world government of some sort is now possible.' Mr. Blainey foresees an attempt to form a world government at some point in the next two centuries, which is an

unusually long time horizon for the average newspaper column.

But—the third point—a change in the political atmosphere suggests that 'global governance' could come much sooner than that. The financial crisis and climate change are pushing national governments towards global solutions, even in countries such as China and the US that are traditionally fierce guardians of national sovereignty.

Virtually the entire intellectual elite of the world realizes that only a centrally operated global authority can guarantee peace, prosperity and security. However, national politicians dare not utter these words because nationalists, by whatever name, are induced to believe that someone, some foreign entity is attempting to steal their country. Thus politicians are careful not to verbalize their intentions. But in the end, they all must come together to fulfill Revelation 17:13: "These have one mind, and shall give their power and strength unto the beast."

The article previously mentioned also contains the following quotes about world government:

[President] Barack Obama, in his book, *The Audacity of Hope*, writes: 'When the world's sole superpower willingly restrains its power and abides by internationally agreed-upon standards of conduct, it sends a message that these rules are worth following.' [. . .] Jacques Attali, an adviser to President Nicolas Sarkozy of France, said: 'Global governance is just a euphemism for global government. . . The core of the international financial crisis is that we have global financial markets and no global rule of law.'

It stands to reason, therefore, that international laws must govern the globe to a much greater extent in the future.

Democracy and Christianity

How democracy is developing and how it affects Christianity, was the subject Samuel J. Andrews wrote about in his book, *Christianity and Anti-Christianity in Their Final Conflict,* published by Moody Press, original copyright 1898. The following are a few excerpts:

It is not to be questioned that social and political conditions have much influence in molding religious opinions, and we assume that the democratic spirit will rule the future. What kind of religious influence is Democracy adapted to exert? In what direction does the democratic current run? According to De Tocqueville, it runs in the direction of very general ideas, and therefore to Pantheism. The idea of the unity of the people as a whole, as one, preponderates, and this extends itself to the world, and to the universe. God and the universe make one whole. This unity has charms for men living in democracies, and prepares them for Pantheistic beliefs. "Among the different systems, by whose aid philosophy endeavors to explain the universe, I believe Pantheism to be one of those most fitted to seduce the human mind in democratic ages; and against it all who abide in their attachment to the true greatness of man, should struggle and combine."

If these remarks of this very acute political observer are true, we may expect to see Pantheism enlarging its influence in

121

Christendom as Democracy extends. (254-55)

Samuel Andrews was not concerned so much about the political development but rather the effects on Christianity.

Under the chapter, "Antichrist as Head of the Nations," he writes:

> More and more all sovereigns and rulers are eager to learn what the wishes of their people are, and careful not to set themselves in direct opposition to them. Whether in the existing monarchies hereditary succession will give place to popular election, is not certain, though it seems probable; but all rulers, hereditary or elected, are made more and more to feel themselves the servants of the people.
>
> This growth of Democracy serves to prepare the way of the Antichrist by making the popular will supreme, both as to the choice of the rulers and the nature and extent of their rule; and by giving legal expression to that will. When a people elects its legislators, the legislation will be what the majority of the voters demand. In the past, among all Christian nations, such legislation has, a great part, been based upon Christian principles, and involved the recognition of God's authority. So long as this authority, as declared in the Scriptures or by the Church, is recognized, the popular will is not supreme; but according as it is denied, this supremacy is more and more enlarged. If, then, the belief become general, either that there is no God, the Lawgiver, or no expression of His will which is authoritative, what principle shall determine the character and limitations of legislation? The only principle is that of the public good; whatever this

demands, is right. If, for example, the law of marriage given in the Bible is set aside as without authority, what shall determine what the new law shall be? It must be what the welfare of society demands, and this is a matter of popular judgment. (264-65)

Very plainly, what is good for the people and for the nation is going to become the final authority. The popular will of the people will become Law!

He then writes:

> *Democracy has enveloped Churchianity to such an extent that it has become impossible to recognize a distinct difference between the world and the church.*

We have reason to believe that, although the practical rejection of all now recognized Divine law may be gradual, the popular supremacy, based upon the public good, will at last be affirmed as absolute in all matters pertaining to man's welfare.

As Democracy makes the popular will supreme, so it provides in general suffrage the legal means of its expression. It is possible that, as regards rulers, this may find its last and highest illustration in the choice between Christ and the Antichrist. As at the end of the Lord's earthly life the Jews were called upon, in a way which we must regard as providential (Matthew 27:15), to choose between Him and Barabbas; so again will He be presented before the covenant peoples—the Christian nations—not indeed as personally present, that they may choose between Him and the Lawless One. The choice of the Antichrist is not to be the choice of the rulers only, or of the popular leaders, the multitude being unwilling, and silent, and passive; it is the act of the peoples, the direct or indirect expression of the popular will. It is the voluntary declaration of Christendom. (266)

> *Europe, the world's leading continent and the most diverse, is unifying, thereby establishing a model for the rest of the world.*

Democracy has enveloped Churchianity to such an extent that it has become impossible to recognize a distinct difference between the world and the church. The popular will of the people is the law!

The Unifying European Union

The success of the European Union can no longer be denied. The EU, without firing a shot, is growing larger and larger, taking on one nation after another.

Thus, the natural question arises: Will Europe enlarge beyond its border? Turkey, not a European nation, has been waiting patiently for over two decades to become a member. A recent poll in Israel revealed that over 70 percent of Israelis would favor membership in the European Union.

In the meantime, the Mediterranean Union has become a prominent movement. At a meeting in 2008, initiated by the French President Sarkozy, all Mediterranean countries (with the exception of Libya) participated, expressing their desire for a closer relationship. What we are seeing today is unprecedented in history. Europe, the world's leading continent and the most diverse, is unifying, thereby establishing a model for the rest of the world.

> ✎ *They are solidly glued together by democracy, socialism, communism, economy, and finances.*

Furthermore, European social democracy has led the continent to be the biggest economy in the world. It is the largest market for import and export. Europe is considered to be the most peaceful and secure continent on earth. All without firing a shot! We must keep in mind that during the last century (1900s), Europe was the center of history's two global wars. Some estimates say that over 100 million people perished during these two wars. But look at Europe today: there is virtually no chance for a war to erupt among the European nations. They are solidly glued together by democracy, socialism, communism, economy, and finances. Are we seeing the fulfillment of Revelation 17:13: "These have one mind"? It is definitely the beginning.

The following is another example of Europe's dominion:

Brussels Writes Global Law

Mark Schapiro—an American investigative journalist of

some twenty years' standing and the editorial director of the Center for Investigative Journalism—believes that we can date the eclipse of the United States by the European Union quite precisely indeed—25 June 2004.

On that day, some 200 million Europeans went to the polls to elect their representatives to the European Parliament, consolidating the union's ascendancy. Europe's parliament leapfrogged the US Congress in size of population represented, with an additional two member states, Romania and Bulgaria, boosting the numbers still further to almost half a billion people in 2007. Even more critically, in 2005, the GDP of the EU overtook that of the States.

"The EU is now the single largest trading partner with every continent except Australia," he writes in his recent book, *Exposed,* which considers the massive global economic power shift that has occurred as a result of these changes. He looks at how companies and state governments in the US, China and the rest of the world increasingly take their legislative lead—whether willingly or dragged kicking and screaming—on issues such as environmental standards, health and safety regulation and consumer protection not from Washington, but Brussels.

The book looks particularly at the effect on American firms of EU legislation such as REACH, Registration, Evaluation, Authorization and Restriction of Chemical substances—the world's strictest chemicals regulatory framework, and RoHS—the Removal of Hazardous Substances directive, as well as moves in the realms of genetically modified organisms, endocrine disruptors in plastics and Europe's embrace of

126

the precautionary principle.

"With wealth comes trade, and from trade comes the power to write the rules of commerce," he announces.

-euobserver.com, 16 July 2008

(*Midnight Call*, March 2009)

Europe the Lawgiver

Regulations for industry and products are written in Brussels, Belgium. The world court is firmly established in The Hague, Netherlands. Any country wanting to deal globally must adhere to EU rules and laws. How are they established? By democracy. Only a few decades ago, it was impossible to imagine that these nations— so diverse in history, language, culture, custom, tradition, even religion—could nevertheless sit at one table and come to an agreement. That is indeed mind-boggling. It is racing toward political globalism.

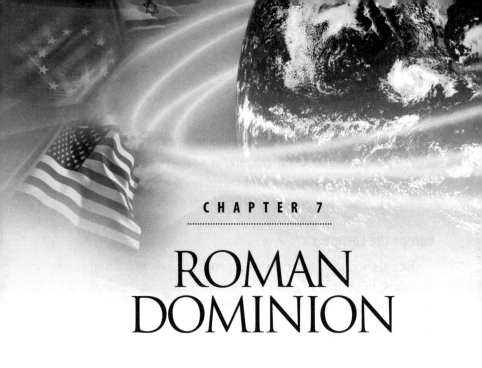

CHAPTER 7

ROMAN DOMINION

About the final Gentile superpower Daniel wrote: "And the fourth kingdom shall be strong as iron: forasmuch as iron breaketh in pieces and subdueth all things; and as iron that breaketh all these, shall it break in pieces and bruise" (Daniel 2:40). Is the European Union the manifestation of the final Gentile power?

Freedom Under Rome

When speaking of ancient Rome, most of us have been strongly influenced by Hollywood, depicting the Roman occupation as brutal and oppressive. The Roman government was hated by all the nations they had occupied. The Romans forced those they conquered into subjection. That is generally accepted. But is that really true? Not according to Scripture.

Here are some examples. When Jesus came to Capernaum, there was a certain centurion (Roman) who had a sick servant, apparently near death. This man sent for Jesus, "beseeching him that he would come and heal his servant"(Luke 7:3). When they came to Jesus, the Jews testified, "For he [the Roman centurion] loveth our nation, and he hath built us a synagogue" (Luke 7:5). This statement in Holy Scripture clearly reveals that a civilized and well-nurtured relationship existed between the Jews who were conquered and the Romans who were the conquerors.

This centurion, the conqueror, debased himself by sending for Jesus, asking for help for the sake of his sick servant. Would your employer do that for you? Most likely not. If you were absent from work for a few weeks or a month, you would probably lose your job. Here we see compassion in action. The people testify of the excellent relationship between the Roman military force and the Jewish people in the land of Israel: "he loveth our nation."

Another instance is recorded of a man in Caesarea named Cornelius, a Roman centurion. The Apostle Peter received this report about him: "And they said, Cornelius the centurion, a just man, and one that feareth God, and of good report among all the nation of the Jews, was warned from God by an holy angel to send for thee into his house, and to hear words of thee" (Acts 10:22). Note it does not say that he had a good report "among some of the Jews," but "among all the nation of the Jews." With these words we receive another clear picture of the relationship between the Jews and the occupying Romans. Cornelius the Roman had a "good report among all the nation of the Jews."

Civil Rights

What about civil rights? Here again, Rome is unmatched in history.

Let us take a look at Acts 22. The Apostle Paul preaches to the Jews in Jerusalem. When he testifies that the Lord told him, "I will send thee far hence unto the Gentiles," the Jews are enraged and ready to kill Paul.

> *The Roman captain ordered 470 soldiers for the protection and safe journey of one Jew!*

The captain of the Roman army, who was made aware of the commotion, could have said, "What is one Jew to us? We have other things to do." Yet, he sent his soldiers to rescue Paul from the Jews, not knowing that Paul was a Roman citizen.

Later, we read that the Roman captain spared no cost to deliver Paul to the proper authority, the governor in Caesarea: "And he called unto him two centurions, saying, Make ready two hundred soldiers to go to Caesarea, and horsemen threescore and ten, and spearmen two hundred, at the third hour of the night; And provide them beasts, that they may set Paul on, and bring him safe unto Felix the governor" (Acts 23:23-24).

We may not fully realize this immense undertaking to save one Jew. The Roman captain ordered 470 soldiers for the protection and safe journey of one Jew! They had to travel about 100 kilometers, and that would take three, four, even five days. Can you imagine the cost to feed the soldiers, with all the helpers and the animals? This was a gigantic undertaking to save one Jew! Do you think your government would do that for you?

These few biblical examples should suffice to document that Israel's relationship to Rome can be considered at least good, if not very good. It is not surprising that 70 percent of Israelis today favor membership in the European Union.

The Shadow of Democracy

Roman Democracy, which is active throughout the world today, also has a shadow side.

We all know the story from reading the Gospels. Jesus was betrayed and arrested. The apparent charge against Him was His title, "King of the Jews." This was a clever maneuver by the religious authorities, who were not authorized to implement capital punishment by crucifixion. So they used a political ploy. The accusation was that Jesus had declared Himself to be the King of the Jews. That would be open rebellion against the Roman government. They alone had the authority to install a king in Israel.

When the Jews had delivered Jesus to the political authority, Pilate, the first question he asked was, "Art thou the King of the Jews?" How did Jesus answer? "Thou sayest it." A rather strange answer. Jesus does not say "yes" or "no." Why not? Because this question was only for the Jews and by the Jews, not for Gentiles, in this case Pilate the Roman. He virtually ignores the question by simply telling Pilate, "You said it."

Democracy Votes for Barabbas

Next we see democracy in action: "And there was one named Barabbas, which lay bound with them that had made insurrection with him, who had committed murder in the insurrection. And the multitude crying aloud began to desire him to do as he had ever done unto them" (Mark 15:7-8). The multitude represents the majority, which is the foundation of democracy.

> The multitude represents the majority, which is the foundation of democracy.

From the next verse, it is apparent that Pilate accepted the title "King of the Jews." Here is what we read in verse 9: "But Pilate answered them, saying, Will ye that I release unto you the King of the Jews?" Pilate was playing politics. The people, under the influence of the religious authority, lobbied their message loud and clear: "But the chief priests moved the people, that he should rather release Barabbas unto them" (verse 11). The Roman governor was playing his game well; he had the crowd on his side, "And

> ✎ The words, "willing to content the people" are the fuel for democracy. The people must get what they want.

Pilate answered and said again unto them, What will ye then that I shall do unto him whom ye call the King of the Jews?" (verse 12). The next three verses determine the crucifixion: "And they cried out again, Crucify him. Then Pilate said unto them, Why, what evil hath he done? And they cried out the more exceed-

> ✎ There is little doubt that mass democracy was the deciding factor used against Jesus to justify the crucifixion of the Son of God.

ingly, Crucify him. And so Pilate, willing to content the people, released Barabbas unto them, and delivered Jesus, when he had scourged him, to be crucified" (verses 13-15). The words, "willing to content the people" are the fuel for democracy. The people must get what they want.

Even on the way to crucifixion, the people mocked Him, "And began to salute him, Hail, King of the

Jews!" (verse 18). And finally, a written documentation was placed over the cross: "And the superscription of his accusation was written over, THE KING OF THE JEWS" (verse 26).

There is little doubt that mass democracy was the deciding factor used against Jesus to justify the crucifixion of the Son of God.

Democracy's History

In the meantime, democracy is literally flooding planet Earth. There are only a few nations left that do not accept democracy as the legitimate way for a government to operate. Sooner or later, most, if not all nations of the world will have to follow in the footsteps of global democracy. What will happen to some of the nations who reject democracy? China is the answer. This communist nation is considered a full-fledged member of the global family of nations without being a democratic nation.

It is helpful to realize that democracy is not a new idea or something that has become popular just lately; democracy is ancient. The word "democracy" derives from the ancient Greek *dimokratia,* which simply means popular government. It consists of *demos*, "the people" and *kratos,* meaning "rules" or "strength." This political system was visibly demonstrated during a popular uprising in Athens in 508 B.C. From that point on, some form of democracy was practiced in many parts of the world. However, democracy is not stationary; it is a revolutionary system that continues to be subject to change by the people, for the people and their respective governments.

Let's take a look at portions of an article in today's popular encyclopedia, Wikipedia, under "Democracy in Ancient Rome":

Birth of the Republic

The traditional founding of Rome was in 753 BC. The Etruscans, early Italian settlers comprised of city-states throughout central Italy ruled Rome for over a century; the traditional dates are 616 BC for the accession of the first Etruscan King, Tarquinius Priscus, and 510 BC for the expulsion of the last king, Tarquinius Superbus.

Roman Kings were elected from each of Rome's major tribes in turn. The exact nature of the king's power is uncertain. He may have held near-absolute power, or may also have merely been the chief executive of the Senate and the people. At least in military matters, the king's authority was likely absolute. He was also the head of the state religion. In addition to the authority (*Imperium*) of the King, there were three administrative assemblies: the Senate, which acted as an advisory body for the King; the Comitia Curiata, which could endorse and ratify laws suggested by the King; and the Comitia Calata, which was an assembly of the priestly college which could assemble the people in order to bear witness to certain acts, hear proclamations, and declare the feast and holiday schedule for the next month.

The class struggles of the Roman Republic resulted in an unusual mixture of democracy and oligarchy. The word republic

135

comes from the Latin *res publica* which literally translates to public business. Roman laws traditionally could only be passed by a vote of the Popular assembly (Comitia Tributa). Likewise, candidates for public positions had to run for election by the people. However, the Roman Senate represented an oligarchic institution, which acted as an advisory body. In the Republic, the Senate held great authority (*auctoritas*), but no actual legislative power; it was technically only an advisory council. However, as the Senators were individually very influential, it was difficult to accomplish anything against the collective will of the Senate. New Senators were chosen from among the most accomplished patricians by Censors (*Censura*), who could also remove a Senator from his office if he was found "morally corrupt"; a charge that could include bribery or, as under Cato the Elder, embracing one's wife in public. Later, under the reforms of the dictator Sulla, Quaestors were made automatic members of the Senate, though most of his reforms did not survive.

New provinces brought wealth to Italy, and fortunes were made through mineral concessions and enormous slave run estates. Slaves were imported to Italy and wealthy landowners soon began to buy up and displace the original peasant farmers. By the late 2nd Century this led to renewed conflict between the rich and poor and demands from the latter for reform of constitution. The background of social unease and the inability of the traditional republican constitutions to adapt to the needs of the growing empire led to the rise of a series of over-mighty generals, championing the cause of either the rich or the poor, in the last century BC.

This description shows that democracy is a rather ancient form of government, by the people and for the people, but not all people were included in the democratic process.

Progressive Democracy

Although democracy was the driving force during the time of the Declaration of Independence in America, it was a very limited democracy. From the approximately four million people living in the country, only about 100,000 had the right to vote. In plain words, this right was reserved for the well-to-do landowners. Ironically, many of these landowners received the land from the Monarch of England, against whom they rebelled.

Women, for example, were not allowed to vote until 1920. Blacks were not considered full human beings. When we keep these facts in mind, then the words we find in the Declaration of Independence sound rather hollow for those who did not have the right as citizens: "We hold these truths to be self-evident, that all men are created equal, that they are endowed by the Creator with certain inalienable rights, that among these are life, liberty and the pursuit of happiness."

> *Voting rights for all people is an evolutionary process and has now become a global force.*

137

Today all that has changed. Democracy makes all people equal, but it was accomplished progressively, and we must add, this is not yet the end.

Voting rights for all people, as we have already said, is an evolutionary process and has now become a global force. Democracy is the key for the nations wanting to experience the well-being of the progressive nations of the world.

Global Interdependency

One thing is becoming crystal clear: We are living in a global world. The nations are becoming more and more interdependent; therefore, it stands to reason that the ultimate answer for mankind is to subject themselves to international law under a globally recognized government, in order to fulfill Scriptures such as Revelation 18:3, "For all nations have drunk of the wine of the wrath of her fornication, and the kings of the earth have committed fornication with her, and the merchants of the earth are waxed rich through the abundance of her delicacies." Democracy will lead to the establishment of universal democracy under the auspices of one great leader, and that is the Antichrist.

> *Democracy is the key for the nations wanting to experience the well-being of the progressive nations of the world.*

138

Multiple Ways to Global Unity

While a universal democracy will be established, we must allow for the possibility of various levels of democracy, incorporating major principals of socialism, communism, and some type of monarchy. Although the European Union (Rome) is built upon the foundation of equality, all levels of democracy can be accommodated.

We must keep in mind that for 6,000 years, Satan has attempted to establish this one world unity in order to challenge the coming 1,000-year Kingdom of Peace of our Lord, but Satan's ways and means are diametrically opposed to the Lord's.

The Bible teaches very plainly and emphatically that there is only one way, and that is the person Jesus Christ. "Jesus saith unto him, I am the way, the truth, and the life: no man cometh unto the Father, but by me" (John 14:6). The devil, however, accepts any and all ways to come to him, no matter what religion or no religion. It makes no difference what nationality, color or race you are, and political practice is not decisive either. All nations will and must come under the authority of Antichrist. So in conclusion of this chapter, we again quote the sentence of Revelation 13:3: "And all the world wondered after the beast."

PART II

RACING TOWARD ECONOMIC GLOBALISM

We have already learned that political globalism is today a reality. There are some dissenters, but they are expected to fall in line sooner or later. Stronger and more powerful than political globalism is economic globalism. This is no longer theory but reality. No nation can act independently to seek its own advantage: the global economic family is now in charge.

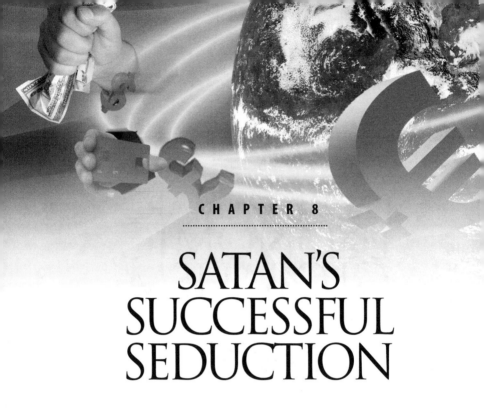

CHAPTER 8

SATAN'S SUCCESSFUL SEDUCTION

Economy is the keystone to globalization. Without the incentive of financial advantage, virtually no nation would be interested in another. As we will see in this chapter, economy is not an isolated issue, but is connected to politics and religion. Our text chapter, Revelation 13, clearly reveals this trinity: politics, commerce and religion.

Global Control

Global economy will ultimately lead to total financial control. Today, we realize that the goal of truly economic globalism is not far off in the distance but is already practiced and is self-evident on virtually all levels of society.

> *All nations are integrated into a financial economic infrastructure, which can no longer be disassembled.*

Where will it lead? "And he causeth all, both small and great, rich and poor, free and bond, to receive a mark in their right hand, or in their foreheads: And that no man might buy or sell, save he that had the mark, or the name of the beast, or the number of his name" (Revelation 13:16-17). Keep in mind when reading this part of the book that all the developments aim toward the fulfillment of that Scripture.

During the financial chaos that emerged in September 2008, it became apparent that no nation is truly independent and that all nations are integrated into a financial economic infrastructure, which can no longer be disassembled. The symbol of capitalism (U.S.A.) and the symbol of communism (China) have become "inseparable twins." These two diverse nations, even divided geographically by the Pacific Ocean, have become dependent on each other, linked by global economy.

Global Recession

Even the skeptics must now agree that we are living in a global world. As the world turns, so do troubles.

When the sun rises in the East—Australia, Japan, Korea, China, etc.—the business day begins. Whatever happens there will affect to some degree Europe in about eight hours. A few hours later, the day begins with South, Central and North America. Everyone does his or her own thing it seems, but in reality, each one depends

> ✎ *Today the world functions like a gigantic assembly line.*

upon the other. Today the world functions like a gigantic assembly line. When something goes wrong anywhere in the world, everyone is going to be affected sooner or later. That is what racing toward economic globalism is all about.

At the time of writing, 18 December 2008, the following selected headlines appeared in the prestigious publication, *Financial Times:*

Slowboat from China
Dollar plunges
Goldman partner's bonuses fall by 80%
Venezuela loses steam
Opec cut falls flat
Honda to cut dividend and management pay
Deutsche takes penalty
Rouble weakens

These are just a few selected items in one daily newspaper, showing how real globalism affects all of us anywhere in the world.

One need not be an expert in finances and economy to realize that something went terribly wrong during 2008 and into 2009.

Global Rearrangement

What is the real reason behind the economic and financial commotion? Nothing other than the rearrangement of capitalism, socialism and communism. When everything is over, and all has been said and done, we will find ourselves in a more regulated and internationally controlled world ... a world in accordance with the desires of man's heart: peace, security and prosperity.

> *When everything is over, and all has been said and done, we will find ourselves in a more regulated and internationally controlled world ... a world in accordance with the desires of man's heart: peace, security and prosperity.*

Here is how Martin Wolf of the *Financial Times* sees it:

Seeds of Its Own Destruction

Another ideological god has failed. The assumptions that ruled policy and politics over three decades suddenly look as outdated as revolutionary socialism.

"The nine most terrifying words in the English language are:

145

'I'm from the government and I'm here to help.'" Thus quipped Ronald Reagan, hero of US conservatism. The remark seems ancient history now that governments are pouring trillions of dollars, euros and pounds into financial systems.

The legitimacy of the market will weaken. The credibility of the US will be damaged. The authority of China will rise. Globalisation itself may founder. This is a time of upheaval.

In the US, core of the global market economy and center of the current storm, the aggregate debt of the financial sector jumped from 22 per cent of gross domestic product in 1981 to 117 per cent by the third quarter of 2008. In the UK, with its heavy reliance on financial activity, gross debt of the financial sector reached almost 250 per cent of GDP.

By intervening to keep their exchange rates down and accumulating foreign currency reserves, governments of emerging economies generated huge current account surpluses, which they recycled, together with inflows of private capital, into official capital outflows: between the end of the 1990s and the peak in July 2008, their currency reserves alone rose by $5,300bn.

These huge flows of capital, on top of the traditional surpluses of a number of high-income countries and the burgeoning surpluses of oil exporters, largely ended up in a small number of high-income countries and particularly in the US. At the peak, America absorbed about 70 per cent of the rest of the world's surplus savings.

Meanwhile, inside the US the ratio of household debt to GDP rose from 66 per cent in 1997 to 100 per cent a decade later. Even bigger jumps in household indebtedness occurred in the UK. These surges in household debt were supported, in turn, by

146

highly elastic and innovative financial systems and, in the US, by government programmes.

We are witnessing the deepest, broadest and most dangerous financial crisis since the 1930s. As Profs Reinhart and Rogoff argue in another paper, "banking crises are associated with profound declines in output and employment." This is partly because of overstretched balance sheets: in the US, overall debt reached an all-time peak of just under 350 per cent of GDP – 85 per cent of it private. This was up from just over 160 per cent of it private. This was up from just over 160 per cent in 1980.

The proposition that sophisticated modern finance was able to transfer risk to those best able to manage it has failed.

The paradigm is, instead, that risk has been transferred to those least able to understand it. As Mr. Volcker remarked during a speech last April: "Simply stated, the bright new financial system – for all its talented participants, for all its rich rewards – has failed the test of the marketplace."

The ability of the west in general and the US in particular to influence the course of events will also be damaged. The collapse of the western financial system, while China's flourishes, marks a humiliating end to the "unipolar moment." As western policymakers struggle, their credibility lies broken. Who still trusts the teachers?

On June 19 2007, I concluded an article on the "new capitalism" with the observation that it remained "untested." The test has come: it failed. The era of financial liberalisation has ended. Yet, unlike in the 1990s, no credi-

ble alternative to the market economy exists and the habits
of international co-operation are deep.

-*Financial Times*, 9 March 2009, pg. 7

This analysis should reinforce our statement that the
world is racing toward economic globalism.

The Dream of Freedom

Since the beginning, it has always been man's dream
to live in peace with one another, to enjoy the labor of
one's hand, to live without fear of losing everything, or
being invaded by a foreign power and becoming subject
to foreign laws, rules and regulations.

Man wants to be free and independent, but each on
his own terms. That is where the world's conflict begins.
Where will it end? Surrendering your freedom and independence to one, the Antichrist.

Satan's Victory March

As we follow this progressive development, we
should keep in mind and be alert to what is really happening. We must not permit ourselves to be confused by
the diverse reports of the media; they are always based
on short-term views. In the long term, it is the preparation for a peaceful world. This is an imitation of the
promised 1,000-year peace, which will be established
by no one but the Prince of Peace, Jesus Christ our
Lord. In the meantime, Satan is planning his victory
march, which will be initiated by the New World Order.

So let's answer the question: Will the New World Order replace a nation's sovereignty?

> The New World Order is not an institution, but a definition of global activity and its respective philosophy, expressing new goals and intentions. Sovereign nations will continue to exist. How do we know? The Bible says that the nations will be judged in accordance with their relationship to Israel. National representatives will come to Jerusalem in the 1,000-year kingdom of peace.
>
> Meanwhile, all nations will become dependent upon the New World Order. The Bible makes it clear that a world government will be established.
>
> Therefore, it is a mistake to assume that the New World Order is exclusively expressed through the United Nations, the Trilateral Commission, the Bilderbergers, the Club of Rome or the European Union. The New World Order can best be defined as a progressive, spiritual movement to establish unity among the nations through diversity in the endtimes.
>
> *(119 Most Frequently Asked Questions About Prophecy,*
> 106-107)

The Master Plan

Before we go into further detail as to the events that are taking place in our world, let us first of all look at the ultimate authority, the prophetic Scripture, which clearly reveals the past, present and future.

> And he exerciseth all the power of the first beast before

him, and causeth the earth and them which dwell therein to worship the first beast, whose deadly wound was healed. And he doeth great wonders, so that he maketh fire come down from heaven on the earth in the sight of men, And deceiveth them that dwell on the earth by the means of those miracles which he had power to do in the sight of the beast; saying to them that dwell on the earth, that they should make an image to the beast, which had the wound by a sword, and did live. And he had power to give life unto the image of the beast, that the image of the beast should both speak, and cause that as many as would not worship the image of the beast should be killed. And he causeth all, both small and great, rich and poor, free and bond, to receive a mark in their right hand, or in their foreheads: And that no man might buy or sell, save he that had the mark, or the name of the beast, or the number of his name. Here is wisdom. Let him that hath understanding count the number of the beast: for it is the number of a man; and his number is Six hundred threescore and six (Revelation 13:12-18).

The endtime scenario described in these verses is one of the most used passages in prophecy-related material. It reveals the final stages in world politics, economy and religion. This is the ultimate result of man's free will, but subjected to the authority of Satan.

There are two points necessary to specifically emphasize:

1. The playing field is planet Earth—that is glob-

alism.

2. Deception.

This is worldwide, whether Churchianity, Islam, Hinduism, Buddhism, atheism, you name it. All are included.

This second beast, the propaganda minister for Antichrist, is the driving force. What is the aim? "To worship the first beast." How does he accomplish it? "He deceiveth them that dwell on the earth."

How is it possible for this man to cause the entire world to worship the image of the beast? Let's read again verse 13: "And he doeth great wonders, so that he maketh fire come down from heaven on the earth in the sight of men" (Revelation 13:13). Remember, fire from heaven.

The Lord God Versus Baal

We are reminded here of the great prophet Elijah, who made fire come down from heaven in the land of Israel. Elijah challenged apostate Israel under the leadership of King Ahab and Jezebel. He courageously confronted King Ahab, who was represented by 450 prophets of Baal and 400 prophets who ate at Jezebel's table. Here is the event:

> And Elijah came unto all the people, and said, How long halt ye between two opinions? if the LORD be God, follow him: but if Baal, then follow him. And the people answered him not a word. Then said Elijah unto the people, I, even I only, remain

a prophet of the LORD; but Baal's prophets are four hundred and fifty men. Let them therefore give us two bullocks; and let them choose one bullock for themselves, and cut it in pieces, and lay it on wood, and put no fire under: and I will dress the other bullock, and lay it on wood, and put no fire under: And call ye on the name of your gods, and I will call on the name of the LORD: and the God that answereth by fire, let him be God. And all the people answered and said, It is well spoken (1 Kings 18:21-24).

> *It was a total sacrifice, and it resulted in total acceptance: the fire of the Lord came from heaven.*

The people present were in full agreement with Elijah's proposal: "It is well spoken." The prophets of Baal were first in line, but without success. "And it came to pass, when midday was past, and they prophesied until the time of the offering of the evening sacrifice, that there was neither voice, nor any to answer, nor any that regarded" (verse 29). Idols don't answer: they are a deception.

Fire From Heaven

Now comes Elijah's turn:

And it came to pass at the time of the offering of the evening sacrifice, that Elijah the prophet came near, and said, LORD God of Abraham, Isaac, and of Israel, let it be known this day

152

that thou art God in Israel, and that I am thy servant, and that I have done all these things at thy word. Hear me, O LORD, hear me, that this people may know that thou art the LORD God, and that thou hast turned their heart back again. Then the fire of the LORD fell, and consumed the burnt sacrifice, and the wood, and the stones, and the dust, and licked up the water that was in the trench (verses 36-38).

That was the visible manifestation of God's acceptance of Elijah's sacrifice.

Elijah Knew God

Had Elijah special faith to believe that things would work out that way? Was he some kind of super-person? Not at all. We find the answer to his confidence revealed in his prayer, "I am thy servant ... I have done all these things at thy word." The Word of God was the foundation of his actions. It was a total sacrifice, and it resulted in total acceptance: the fire of the Lord came from heaven.

Most of us are familiar with the detailed story recorded in 1 Kings 18 and 19. This visible demonstration caused the confession of the people, "And when all the people saw it, they fell on their faces: and they said, The LORD, he is the God; the LORD, he is the God" (1 Kings 18:39).

Endtime Fire From Heaven

Now in the end stages of the end times, we see the false prophet being able to perform "great wonders, so that he maketh fire come down from heaven on the earth." Some scholars have interpreted this to mean a nuclear bomb. Others say it's the fire of the devil. Whatever it is, the people on earth accept this as a great wonder. Under the authority of Satan, this man is able to bring down "fire from heaven." That simply is a fact.

> *The visible manifestation of great wonders and fire from heaven "in the sight of men" is the convincing factor in this work of deception.*

Where is it taking place? "On the earth in the sight of men." Again, this is a visible reality on earth. Twice we read, "them that dwell on the earth" in verse 14. They are deceived because of miracles. In this case the visible manifestation of great wonders and fire from heaven "in the sight of men" is the convincing factor in this work of deception.

We can well imagine that the news media will proclaim in large letters and via television this great event in order to establish these miracles as the testimony to the authority of the false prophet. He apparently operates with supernatural powers. This man also has the power that causes man to worship the beast. He causes the death of those who would not worship the image of the beast, and he causes the implementation of the mark of the beast.

Buy and Sell

Economy can only function by the exchange mechanism of buying and selling. Once you stop buying and selling, you will cease to exist. In other words, it's impossible to do without buying and selling. There simply cannot be a capitalist, socialist or communist economy without buying and selling. That is what the mark of the beast is all about; it is total control.

> With the mark of the beast, particularly with the name of the mark of the beast, Satan seals their eternal condemnation.

We are not going to speculate as to the identity of the mark of the beast—what it is, what it looks like, and how it is applied. There are innumerable theories you can read about in books and on the Internet. We have written two books on this subject, titled, *Preparing for the Mark of the Beast* and *The Coming Digital God,* which elaborate the issue in finer detail. In this book, we will not go further, save to reconfirm that what is written will take place in due time.

Why the Mark of the Beast?

Now it's time to ask an important question: What is the supreme purpose and aim of Satan? After all, he is already in charge of planet Earth; he is called the god of this world. The Bible gives him the legal right to humanity with the words, "He that committeth sin is of the devil." Since all have sinned, all are of the devil. That is a fundamental truth.

So why go through this process that leads to the implementation of the mark of the beast? The answer can be expressed with one word: imitation. What is Satan imitating? He is imitating the seal of the Holy Spirit. With the mark of the beast, particularly with the name of the mark of the beast, Satan seals their eternal condemnation.

This is the imitation of 1 Corinthians 12:13: "For by one Spirit are we all baptized into one body, whether we be Jews or Gentiles, whether we be bond or free; and have been all made to drink into one Spirit." This is the seal of the believer's eternal salvation.

Let us also read Ephesians 1:13: "In whom ye also trusted, after that ye heard the word of truth, the gospel of your salvation: in whom also after that ye believed, ye were sealed with that holy Spirit of promise." This is not accomplished by force, but by faith.

Satan's Promise of Peace

Satan knows too well that he is a defeated foe and that Jesus Christ is the Son of God, who triumphed victoriously over sin, death and the devil. But this simple truth is not accepted by the world. Only a few, the "small flock" receives this truth. The rest of the world, the overwhelming majority, is convinced that man can bring about peace, security, and prosperity by his own works, without the supernatural interference of God. That is exactly what Satan wants. He deceives people by various means. When properly educated and trained, man can live in peace with his fellow man, and therefore is capable of building a peaceful society on planet Earth. That is the reason why every government on earth tells their people: "We are a peaceful, loving nation, and are concerned for the well-being and prosperity of our citizens. We oppose evil and will fight tyranny." These are the proclamations the devil wholeheartedly confirms with his Amen!

Preparation Time

Satan's gospel has been proclaimed since the beginning of man. This is a very important issue to realize when we study the prophetic Word. Too often we place all these events in the distant future. For that reason, many ministers neglect the study and teaching of the prophetic Word, as they say it is future and not for the Church. The Church of Jesus Christ is going to be raptured before these events take place, so why bother with it?

John is the only writer of the Bible who uses the term "Antichrist" in Scripture: "Little children, it is the last time: and as ye have heard that antichrist shall come, even now are there many antichrists; whereby we know that it is the last time" (1 John 2:18). That was written almost 2,000 years ago. Yet John says, "we know that it is the last time." Luther translates it, "we recognize that this is the last hour." Here we clearly see that it is a fatal mistake to place prophecy in the future. The Word of God is a living Word: it is present, applicable for today, just as it was 2,000 years ago. What is often overlooked is the fact that time is needed for preparation.

Daniel Example

We already quoted Daniel 2:44 as an example in chapter 5 of this book, but to drive home the point, let's read it again: "And in the days of these kings shall the God of heaven set up a kingdom, which shall never be destroyed: and the kingdom shall not be left to other people, but it shall break in pieces and consume all these kingdoms, and it shall stand for ever." With the words "these kings" Daniel includes the kingdoms of Babylon, Persia, Greece and Rome. That is a time period of about 2,600 years. Yet he writes, inspired by the Holy Spirit, "in the days of these kings shall the God of heaven set up a kingdom, which shall never be destroyed."

> *Parallel to God's preparation is Satan's preparation to establish his kingdom on earth.*

The visible implementation of this kingdom is yet to come, but already, way back in Nebuchadnezzar's time, God was setting up His "kingdom, which shall never be destroyed," and He is still doing it today.

Parallel to God's preparation is Satan's preparation to establish his kingdom on earth. Today we are witnessing the accelerating preparation for the manifestation of Satan's power on earth.

Lucifer's "I Will"

Satan wants to establish his dominion over mankind in the face of the Lord, the God of heaven and earth. It is none other than an act of rebellion against the Creator.

Let us read what the prophet Isaiah wrote about Satan:

> *This desire for self-benefit, a gospel of prosperity, is in reality the gospel of Satan, and will lead to destruction.*

How art thou fallen from heaven, O Lucifer, son of the morning! how art thou cut down to the ground, which didst weaken the nations! For thou hast said in thine heart, I will ascend into heaven, I will exalt my throne above the stars of God: I will sit also upon the mount of the congregation, in the sides of the north: I will ascend above the heights of the clouds; I will be like the most High (Isaiah 14:12-14).

Notice the "I will" of Satan; he wants to be on par with God.

Today's "I Will" Deception

This diabolical spirit has saturated planet Earth, even Churchianity. It is popular today to preach a gospel that is based on "I will...I must improve my self-esteem...I must have a better marriage...I will have better children...I will fight evil to the betterment of my country." While these desires may be considered good and noble, they contradict the spirit of the New Testament.

Hear the testimony of the Apostle Paul: "For to me to live is Christ, and to die is gain...For I am in a strait betwixt two, having a desire to depart, and to be with Christ; which is far better" (Philippians 1:21, 23). Read also Colossians 3:3: "For ye are dead, and your life is hid with Christ in God."

> *Global economy is the adhesive that glues the nations of the world inseparably together.*

How about Romans 6:6: "Knowing this, that our old man is crucified with him, that the body of sin might be destroyed, that henceforth we should not serve sin." In summary, the self must die! This desire for self-benefit, a gospel of prosperity, is in reality the gospel of Satan, and will lead to destruction.

The Possession Deception

Global economy is the adhesive that glues the nations of the world inseparably together. It is the goal of the nations and of individuals to possess their share of materialism. Possessions, whether it is investments, cash, real estate, or other valuables, are the things of earth we are admonished not to strive after. Actually, James 5:1-3 warns: "Go to now, ye rich men, weep and howl for your miseries that shall come upon you. Your riches are corrupted, and your garments are motheaten. Your gold and silver is cankered; and the rust of them shall be a witness against you, and shall eat your flesh as it were fire. Ye have heaped treasure together for the last days."

We do not need to quote reports of tragedies across the world that occurred recently when large corporations, as well as individuals, suddenly found that most of their possessions were gone. What a fitting statement here in Scripture: "Ye have heaped treasure together for the last days."

Fornication Deception

Twelve times we read the word "fornication" in the Book of Revelation. The first three times are in relation to spiritual idolatry in Revelation 2:14, 20 and 21. Then we read in Revelation 9:21: "Neither repented they of their murders, nor of their sorceries, nor of their fornication, nor of their thefts." This is a different type of fornication. To better understand what this is saying, let us read Revelation 9:20: "And the rest of the men which were not killed by these plagues yet repented not of the works of their hands, that they should not worship devils, and idols of gold, and silver, and brass, and stone, and of wood: which neither can see, nor hear, nor walk." This simply speaks of possessions. The spirit of possessing material things goes so far that they are actually worshiped.

Materialistic Babylon

Next we read in Revelation 14:8: "And there followed another angel, saying, Babylon is fallen, is fallen, that great city, because she made all nations drink of the wine of the wrath of her fornication." Who is this Babylon? Are we to assume that it is ancient literal Babylon, or is it Jerusalem? I believe we are making a mistake if we try to identify a geographical place. As already mentioned in the beginning of this book, the anti-Christian empire is global and cannot be placed in a straightjacket of limited geography.

> *The anti-Christian empire is global and cannot be placed in a straight-jacket of limited geography.*

What we do know is that Rome is the last Gentile superpower, and it is the earthly, physical contact point of Satan and his demonic host.

Spiritual Babylon

In Revelation 13, we read of endtime Babylon: "And there was given unto him a mouth speaking great things and blasphemies; and power was given unto him to continue forty and two months" (verse 5). Again, it is a mistake to isolate this to one certain group or geographical area. What we do know is that Mystery Babylon persecuted the church: "And I saw the woman drunken with the blood of the saints, and with the blood of the martyrs of Jesus: and when I saw her, I wondered with great admiration" (Revelation 17:6). For better understanding, let us read the last sentence in the American Standard Version: "And when I saw her, I wondered with a great wonder."

While Mystery Babylon is global, we do have a topographical reference given in Revelation 17:9: "And here is the mind which hath wisdom. The seven heads are seven mountains, on which the woman sitteth." The beast we read of in Revelation 13 had seven heads, and they are identified as "seven mountains." We already mentioned that Rome is built on seven mountains, but it is necessary to again emphasize that Rome also represents the entire world. Who is Babylon, and who is this woman? Chapter 17, verse 18 gives us the answer: "And the woman which thou sawest is that great city, which reigneth over the kings of the earth."

Only Four Gentile Powers

Who has reigned over the earth? No one except Rome and the previous three Gentile superpowers: Greece, Medo-Persia and Babylon. Only Rome, however, literally and physically dominated planet Earth.

Rome represents Europe, and Europe is responsible for the discovery, the conquering and the establish-

163

ment of the two new continents: America and Australia.

It was the European powers that carved up the American continent (North and South) into 35 nations.

The European colonial powers determined the borders of Africa and divided it into 53 nations. It was Europe who determined to a degree the borders of the 50 nations of Asia. So again, simply put, Mystery Babylon is Rome, Rome is Europe, and Europe represents the world.

Global Materialistic Fornication

Now we should better understand what is written in Revelation 17:2: "With whom the kings of the earth have committed fornication, and the inhabitants of the earth have been made drunk with the wine of her fornication."

Note very specifically what it says in Revelation 18:3: "For all nations have drunk of the wine of the wrath of her fornication, and the kings of the earth have committed fornication with her, and the merchants of the earth are waxed rich through the abundance of her delicacies." The words "all nations," "the kings of the earth," and "the merchants of the earth" clearly describe the global world.

Who made the earth rich? We know that China, or other Asian countries, did not go out into Europe, Africa or America to establish colonies, but Europe did. The same can be said for Africa. No African power went outside the continent to establish their dominion; only Europe did.

The Earth Made Rich

Money, possession and power were the motives behind the spirit of Europe in conquering the continents, so that "the merchants of the earth are waxed rich through the abundance of her delicacies."

When this global economic system, with its mixture of communism, socialism, and capitalism literally evaporates in smoke, we are told in Revelation 18:9: "And the kings of the earth, who have committed fornication and lived deliciously with her, shall bewail her, and lament for her, when they shall see the smoke of her burning."

Therefore, fornication means that man worships his possessions that are made of materials instead of the Creator of the materials. That is the deeper meaning of mystery Babylon.

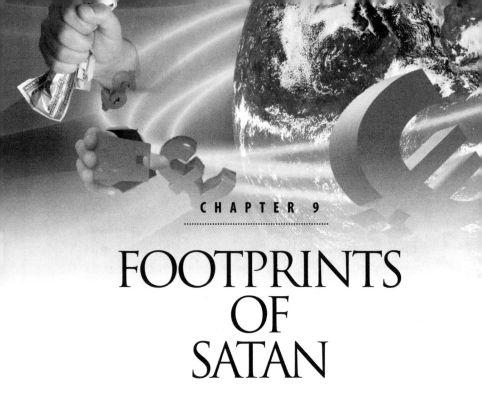

CHAPTER 9

FOOTPRINTS OF SATAN

In order to confirm Satan's authority over planet Earth, his masterpiece, the Antichrist, must establish his powerbase in such a fashion that the world will acknowledge him to be the savior of the world, the redeemer of mankind, and the prince of peace. But the Bible calls him the beast, an animal.

The Beast

Let us review chapter 13 of the book of Revelation again to point out several important issues.

"And I stood upon the sand of the sea, and saw a beast rise up out of the sea, having seven heads and ten horns,

166

and upon his horns ten crowns, and upon his heads the name of blasphemy" (Revelation 13:1). This man is called a beast. Other translations use the word "animal." That is probably a more appropriate translation, because this person, the Antichrist, has totally lost the image of God in which he was created. He now behaves like an animal, without a spirit; thus he is called an animal, a beast.

The Four Beasts

Further we read: "And the beast which I saw was like unto a leopard, and his feet were as the feet of a bear, and his mouth as the mouth of a lion: and the dragon gave him his power, and his seat, and great authority" (verse 2). Here we have three animals: a leopard, a bear, and a lion, but the fourth is not mentioned.

This reminds us of Daniel chapter 7, where the four Gentile superpowers are pictured:

> And four great beasts came up from the sea, diverse one from another. The first was like a lion, and had eagle's wings: I beheld till the wings thereof were plucked, and it was lifted up from the earth, and made stand upon the feet as a man, and a man's heart was given to it. And behold another beast, a second, like to a bear, and it raised up itself on one side, and it had three ribs in the mouth of it between the teeth of it: and they said thus unto it, Arise, devour much flesh. After this I beheld, and lo another, like a leopard, which had upon the back of it four wings of a fowl; the beast had also four heads; and dominion was given to it. After this I saw in the night visions, and behold a fourth beast, dreadful and terrible, and strong

167

> exceedingly; and it had great iron teeth: it devoured and brake in
> pieces, and stamped the residue with the feet of it: and it was
> diverse from all the beasts that were before it; and it had ten horns
> (verses 3-7).

The fourth one is so dreadful and terrible that no animal is found to symbolize it. Revelation simply calls him "the beast."

The Power of the Beast

Revelation 13:3 says: "And I saw one of his heads as it were wounded to death; and his deadly wound was healed: and all the world wondered after the beast." You can't be more globalistic than "all the world." Finally, a man arises out of the sea of nations who is different than all the politicians in the world ... someone who is respected, courageous, well-liked ... a man who is admired by all people, and in the end, even worshiped.

Power Was Given

We already mentioned in chapter 2 that this beast has no power of his own, but this fact needs to be reemphasized. He receives power directly from Satan, as is evident in this chapter: "and the dragon gave him his power" (verse 2); "the dragon which gave power unto the beast" (verse 4); "And there was given unto him a mouth speaking great things and blasphemies; and power was given unto him to continue forty and two months" (verse 5). In verse 7 we read twice that it was given unto him. Note particularly the last sentence: "And power was given him over all kindreds, and tongues, and nations."

We are being introduced to a superhuman; one whom the world loves, adores, and worships, but not by his own power. This is also confirmed in Daniel 8:24: "And his power shall be mighty, but not by his own power: and he shall destroy wonderfully, and shall prosper, and practice, and shall destroy the mighty and the holy people."

Antichrist's success is promoted by the second beast, the false prophet. He puts all his power behind the first beast, with the intention of eliminating all opposition and exercising total control over humanity. That is accomplished through the mark of the beast.

> *Satan must establish a power structure on earth that challenges the absolute power of Jesus Christ the Lord.*

Let us read again Revelation 13:16-17: "And he causeth all, both small and great, rich and poor, free and bond, to receive a mark in their right hand, or in their foreheads: And that no man might buy or sell, save he that had the mark, or the name of the beast, or the number of his name."

The Beast Messiah

Only total control can bring about total power. From Scripture we know that there is only one to whom belongs this power: "And Jesus came and spake unto them, saying, All power is given unto me in heaven and in earth" (Matthew 28:18). That is total and absolute power.

It stands to reason that Satan, with his helpers the Antichrist and false prophet, must establish a power structure on earth that challenges the absolute power of Jesus Christ the Lord. Satan's hidden agenda must include the demonstration of his power globally on the political, economic and religious level.

I think it to be a great error when we try to pinpoint various countries, empires, or religions that will produce this absolute power over planet Earth. Satan, with his team of the Antichrist and false prophet, is in charge of all the nations of the world.

> All of humanity since creation, the whole planet, has become subject to the devil since the fall of man.

Already today they exercise their dominion over the six and a-half billion people on earth.

The Conspiracy Beast

Satan is in control of planet Earth. Not the capitalists, socialists or communists, neither the various movements and organizations such as the Illuminati, the Bilderbergers, the Council of Foreign Relations, the United Nations, the European Union, and innumerable others we do not need to name. They are only tiny specks in the gigantic movement of Satan and the one-third of the fallen angelic hosts.

You may name any important person on planet Earth,

including the President of the United States. They are so little and so insignificant that they barely need mentioning.

When reading the Word of God, we must keep the big picture in mind. All of humanity since creation, the whole planet, has become subject to the devil since the fall of man. There is no escape whatsoever except one way, and that is Jesus who said, "I am the way, the truth, and the life, no man cometh unto the Father but by me" (John 14:6).

A Personal Note

If you are honestly searching for truth, you will find Satan's footprints in your own country, in the very history books

> Don't look too much for the footprints of Satan in other places: look for them at your own doorstep, yes, even your own life.

from which you have been instructed in your schools, as well as in your own churches. Don't look too much for the footprints of Satan in other places: look for them at your own doorstep, yes, even your own life. If you are born again of the Spirit of God, your body is the temple of the Holy Spirit. Has that temple been desecrated by the footprints of Satan? That is the important question we need to ask ourselves constantly.

Who Is to Blame for the Financial Chaos?

We would be shortsighted if we assumed that the present chaos in the financial and commercial world is due to some identifiable political, economic or financial decision-making of any nation. Although it stands to reason that some of those actions were contributing factors toward the result, yet above and beyond, it is always Satan and his plan of deception in making the world believe that he can dethrone the Lord of lords and the King of kings.

When reading and hearing the innumerable commentaries in the media, it is quite evident that the world at large believes they have their destiny in their own hands. They are the masters of this world, and arrogantly proclaim that they will in the end achieve peace, prosperity and security for all people all over the world.

The Culprit

When the financial system started to collapse in the United States in September 2008, there was much *schadenfreude* among European nations. It was clear that America's loosely and often unregulated banking system was the initiating culprit to the near collapse of the financial system.

But it did not take long before the American-initiated financial fiasco spread to other countries, and before a month had passed, virtually the whole world reported near catastrophic decline on all economic and financial levels. This global recession revealed that the world is already solidly united. All that is left for the world is to be governed increasingly by international law. Following is a quote that should reinforce this new global tendency:

Shared Globalism Going Forward

Now that the contagion of financial crisis has rocked the entire world, the calls for greater global coordination are becoming shrill. For example, said Miguel Angel Ordonez, Spain's ECB (European Central Bank) Governor, "We've got to get together on both sides of the Atlantic. It is absolutely essential to co-ordinate everything, including monetary policy."

According to a global financial analyst, "A global conference (along the lines of Bretton Woods) under a respected chairman (Paul Volcker is the obvious choice) must be convened. It would bring together all the major players including the vital creditor nations—China, Japan . . . etc.—to develop a framework for the major economic reforms (currency policies, fiscal disciplines and trade barriers) to work towards a resolution of the crisis."

We can definitely draw several conclusions. First, whatever new global organization emerges, its powers will be shared more equally in the future. Multipolarism must eventually gain ground, according to Bible prophecy. The United States will eventually lose its outsized number of votes and vetoes in such organizations as the International Monetary Fund (IMF) and others. The second conclusion we can safely draw is that we live in a time where an alignment of 10 kings could be on our very doorstep. There is yet one more sure conclusion—a future period of apparent prosperity around the globe, even if only fleeting.

(Wilfred Hahn, *Midnight Call*, February 2009, 14-15)

Easy credit, particularly the unsecured loans for housing, may have been the beginning of the soap bubble's burst, but the continual developments revealed that virtually the entire world banking system was built on a *fairy tale security system*. In biblical language, "the inhabitants of the earth have been made drunk with the wine of her fornication" (Revelation 17:2).

It stands to reason, therefore, that the entire financial system of planet Earth will have to be realigned, reregulated and restructured. No country in the world can allow itself the luxury of independence. All nations are interdependent already.

The Beast of Economic Globalism

Are we in reality racing toward economic globalism? I would think that the answer to that question would be an affirmative "yes" by the overwhelming majority of the people of the world. To be independent of other nations is a thing of the past. No one nation can stand alone. All have been knit together into an interdependent society.

An article from *Yahoo! Finance,* posted 15 September 2008 by Aaron Task, describes America's dependency on nations the U.S. has spurned for so long, but today have become the masters:

Big Risk: Surging Debt Makes U.S. More Dependent on China, Russia, Gulf States

The demise of Lehman Brothers, Merrill Lynch, and Bear Stearns this year has investors contemplating the long-term outlook for other once-venerable institutions, including Dow members Citigroup, AIG and Bank of America.

But there's an even bigger financial institution with greater debt and an increasing level of bad loans on its books: The U.S. government.

Given the actions already taken, from the Housing Bill to the nationalization of Fannie Mae and Freddie Mac, the U.S. deficit could double to $800 billion in two years, says Nouriel Roubini, of NYU's Stern School and RGE Monitor. (Even worse, the official government deficit figures exclude the costs of the wars in Iraq and Afghanistan, as well as the unfunded liabilities of Social Security and Medicare.)

The big risk is that foreign holders of Treasuries will no longer accept low interest rates to help fund U.S. debt spending, says Roubini, noting countries like China, Russia and oil-producing nations in the Middle East have becoming increasingly important holders of Treasuries. Should they demand higher rates to hold U.S. debt or, worse, dump their holdings, it could have profound ramifications on the U.S. economy and the value of the dollar.

It's tempting to dismiss the notion of a "run" on the U.S. government as unthinkable and some bears have been warning for years, even decades, about such a worst-case scenario. But after the events of this weekend, much less the past six months, it's clear that (almost) anything is possible and no scenario too "outrageous" to seriously contemplate.

Is this plain enough?! Communist China has the power in dollars to significantly upset, if not devastate the U.S. economy. In the meantime, socialist Europe is forced to pour billions of euros in support of financial institutions to avoid the meltdown created by the so-called free capitalist enterprises, now on the edge of bankruptcy.

The Beast of Interdependency

Interdependence of all nations is an undeniable reality. It is confirmed in Scripture. The race toward economic globalism is well on its way and will be fully implemented in due time. We may deny it as much as we want, but it will not change anything. The U.S.A., for example, needs the

> *Interdependence of all nations is an undeniable reality.*

rich Chinese communist to lend money [buy U.S. bonds] so the government can continue to function. But China cannot afford to lose the U.S.A. as a customer, now the second biggest behind Japan. Europe cannot afford to be too obnoxious to Russia; otherwise, the much-needed oil and gas pipeline is turned off. Neither can Russia afford losing the hard euro currency to finance its elaborate multi-millionaire club and build up its military force.

The following article describes the reversal of fortune that is now happening in China:

Growing Opportunities for Wealth

The Industrial & Commercial Bank of China [HSBC] has launched private banking services on the mainland, saying it would target customers with net assets of $10m or more with $3m available for investment, who could deposit a minimum of $1m.

The bank estimated there would be more than 16m such potential Chinese customers by 2011 with total assets of more than $6,200bn.

For Bank of China, taking a stake in the Rothschild French private banking operations is intended to provide it with more expertise for its newly wealthy customers. The bank is the country's third-largest lender and the most international by virtue of its history as the official foreign currency handler under the centrally-planned economy of the communist era.

"We remain a Chinese bank," said Min Zhu, Bank of China vice-president for international finance. "We don't want to be a global local bank. We have the market and the growth in China but we don't have the products," he said. Some 80 percent of savings in China are cashbased, he added. "In China individuals are looking for investments and instructions so we want to meet that demand."

"China has been getting most of its technology from Europe—that's the first wave. We see a second wave in which a lot of European mid-cap companies will be ready to sell after one or two generations and will need Chinese co-operation, so there will be big demand in Europe," said Mr. Zhu.

"The Chinese people are ferocious savers," said Robert Agnew of Matrix Services in a recent report on China's investment manage-

The race toward economic globalism is well on its way and will be fully implemented in due time.

ment industry. "They save 40 percent of their incomes and as a result there is at least $2,500bn saved in bank accounts in China. In addition, I have estimated there is an additional $1,200bn of pooled capital being actively managed by institutional investors."

-Financial Times, 19 September 2008, pg. 18

Here is my commentary:

In spite of many setbacks and scandals, China's communist economy is expanding. Suddenly, communism appears in a different light. They are eager to invest globally. But in the end, China too will be disappointed, as all nations of the world. The accumulation of riches contributes to the deafening of spiritual ears and blinding of spiritual eyes. Jesus asked these two questions: "For what is a man profited, if he shall gain the whole world, and lose his own soul? or what shall a man give in exchange for his soul?" (Matthew 16:26).

(*Midnight Call*, December 2008, pg. 38)

Counterfeit Peace

Do we need to say more about racing toward economic globalism? While it is true that this became a reality only during the last few decades, we cannot deny that it was in preparation long ago.

Who prepared it? None other than Satan himself, who desperately seeks his manifestation to the entire world as the prince of this world, the god of this world, the savior of planet Earth. Thus the question, where does it all lead? Answer: The imitation of the 1,000-year Kingdom of Peace is Satan's plan for the world— not the real one, but a counterfeit.

Nor does it matter what the nations have done in the past, who they are, or whatever their goals and aspirations might be. The bottom line is always the conflict between the prince of darkness and the Prince of Light.

Christians in the Last Days

What should our concern be as Christians? What should our actions be? Where do we fit in? Reading the countless pieces of literature I receive on my desk, there are many diverse opinions. It is important to restate that we as Christians are in this world, but not of this world. We may be Americans, Canadians, Russians, Chinese, etc., but that is only temporary. We who believe in the Lord Jesus Christ are purchased with the blood of the Lamb—we are a new nation. The Apostle Peter defines us: "But ye are a chosen generation, a royal priesthood, an holy nation, a peculiar people; that ye should shew forth the praises of him who hath called you out of darkness into his marvellous light" (1 Peter 2:9). It is a tragedy that so many Christians do not realize that they belong to a totally different nation, "a holy nation."

The Invisible Enemy

It is significant that Peter continues to make a remarkable statement: "Which in time past were not a people, but are now the people of God: which had not obtained mercy, but now have obtained mercy" (1 Peter 2:10). This truth is very difficult to accept for nationalists who have

179

been indoctrinated all their life that their nation is the best, the greatest, is superior above all others. Peter actually says, "in time past were not a people." That puts cold water on our national enthusiasm. We are nothing when it comes to our nationality, but then the next seven words are overwhelming, "but are now the people of God."

So what is our task, our fight, our battle? This is what we read in Ephesians 6:12: "For we wrestle not against flesh and blood, but against principalities, against powers, against the rulers of the darkness of this world, against spiritual wickedness in high places." We are to stand against the powers of the invisible world; that is, Satan and his cohorts. Are we to attack? Not at all: we are simply to do one thing, and that is stand. Here is what verse 13 says: "Wherefore take unto you the whole armour of God, that ye may be able to withstand in the evil day, and having done all, to stand."

Satan, the Real Enemy

When we permit ourselves to be confused by the various political and economic systems such as capitalism, socialism and communism, then we are hiding the real enemy, who has these three major systems, including many others, under his total control. We must also remember, "Satan himself is transformed into an angel of light" (2 Corinthians 11:14). To the Christianized European world, he appears in different forms and makeup than he does to the Muslim or the communist world, but it is still the same enemy with the same goal: namely, racing toward global economy.

Irreversible Deception

The continuous process of Satan's deception has definitely accelerated during the last century. It is not a matter of who is right or wrong, or which moral philosophy should have the upper hand; that all plays a secondary role. The progressive and irreversible deception is a natural one.

All of us, whether Christian or non-Christian, rely on the economy. We must work to earn money to support our family.

> *The continuous process of Satan's deception has definitely accelerated during the last century.*

Actually, we are encouraged in the Bible to do so. But allow me to picture the tremendous change that has taken place during the last century. The family unit was made up of husband, wife and children. The husband went to work, and the wife stayed at home, taking care of the children. That was the normal family unit.

How does the family look today? In most cases, both husband and wife must go to work. Increasingly, it is the wife who earns more than the husband; thus, slowly but surely, the role reversal is in progress. As a result, children often rebel. Why? Because the mother was not there when they came home from school. When they were small, they spent much of their time in a childcare center; thus, contact with the parents was reduced substantially. This attention deficit and the lack of family time is a contributing factor toward marital problems. Thus divorce became an accepted alternative. The United States is leading the global divorce rate. What is an even greater tragedy is that divorces are more frequent among evangelical Christians than the rest of the U.S.A.

The Beast of Materialism

What is the cause of this change? One word: materialism. We must have this and that. In order to possess these things, income has to increase; subsequently, a second paycheck becomes essential for a family to function in the modern world.

> *We no longer go to work to earn a living, but we live for the very purpose of working.*

Today, families are more dependent on the economy than ever before. We no longer go to work to earn a living, but we live for the very purpose of working.

Leading in this progression of work to obtain more possessions is the United States of America. Here are some recently published statistics to show how much paid leave the average worker receives among different countries.

182

Average Paid Vacation Days and Holidays (National and Religious) in the Manufacturing Sector Covered by a Collective Bargaining Agreement, 1999

	Vacation Days	Holidays (Natl. and Religious)	Total Days of Paid Leave
Italy	37	8	45
Finland	37.5	7	44.5
Netherlands	31	7.1	38.1
Germany	30	8	38
Luxembourg	28	10	38
Austria	26.5	9.5	36
Portugal	22	14	36
Spain	22	14	36
Denmark	27	7	34
France	25	9	34
Sweden	25	9	34
United Kingdom	25	9	34
Switzerland	24.3	9	33.3
Belgium	20	11	31
Greece	22	9	31
Japan	18	13	31
Ireland	21	9	30
Norway	21	7	28
United States	12	11	23

Source: The Confederation of German Employers' Associations, unpublished data, 1999.

Data on collective bargaining agreements in the manufacturing sector show that European workers often receive more paid leave (holidays and vacation) than the legally mandated number of days.

Work for a Living or Live for Work?

Many experts agree that there is a relationship between

the functionality of the family and overworked parents.

One thing becomes clear, and this applies to socialist Europe as well: The dependency on work is increasing year-by-year. Instead of attaining more freedom, we are becoming more dependent on our workplace. While the industrial revolution and the following technological inventions have made physical labor easier, it definitely did not result in more freedom for the average family.

Speaking of freedom, what is freedom? If you were to ask that question to a number of nationals, you would receive diverse answers. Americans have their own way of determining freedom, which, for example, the French would not accept; thus, we must not be narrowminded and accept our definition of freedom to be applicable to the world.

Threefold Definition of Freedom

A research paper I read many years ago had this to say:

> A man divides his 24 hours into 8-hour sections. He sleeps 8 hours, stays at home 8 hours, and works 8 hours. When he sleeps, he enjoys freedom, no matter where he resides in the world. When he is in his house, that freedom has to be shared with his family, and quite often to a degree with neighbors. Thus freedom becomes limited. Then he goes to work. At that point, freedom is totally lost. He is not free to do as he pleases, to say what he wants, or express his sense of freedom in any way, shape, or form. He has now surrendered his freedom to his employer.

(Source unknown)

184

This illustration carries profound truths, but it leaves one thing out: the true freedom which believers have in Jesus Christ. Those who have surrendered all to Him are totally free.

Depression of 1929

There are still some people alive today who recall the times of the Great Depression.

I asked my mother (born 18 December 1909) what the experience was like during the Great Depression in Germany. She answered, "I never noticed there was one." The recession and subsequent depression were felt by those who were racing toward more possessions, more money and more riches. But the rest of the people, mainly agrarian workers, had little to no relationship to the business world. They were not involved, and therefore were not much affected by it all.

Today, it is a totally different story. The farming community has shrunk to about 1.5 to 2 percent of the population in the progressive nations. Because of advanced technology, they too are very dependent on the economy, financial institutions and the global price war. Virtually no one is exempt: all are part of the race for more material possessions. That is the picture of today. For the first time, the whole world is affected by the global economic recession.

The Love of Money

Finally, we are reminded of the words of 1 Timothy

6:10: "For the love of money is the root of all evil: which while some coveted after, they have erred from the faith, and pierced themselves through with many sorrows." The love of money is the key to possessions and materialism. We also learn that the loss of possessions for those who love money is considered to be the greatest tragedy. Revelation chapter 18, verse 17: "For in one hour so great riches is come to naught."

CHAPTER 10

THE
BEAST
OF
PROSPERITY

According to the prophet Daniel, we are living in the final kingdom. It is the time period marked by the kingdom made up of iron and clay. The previous three kingdoms were represented by brass (Greece), silver (Medo-Persia) and gold (Babylon). While gold and silver are rare, iron and clay can be found in abundance all over planet Earth; in other words, they are not very valuable. These definitions, however, are viewed from God's perspective. It does not mean that Babylon was the richest and our democratic world is the poorest; the opposite is true. Under democracy, the world has been enriched as never before. When we compare the times of the Babylonian kingdom with today's world, we would definitely come to the conclusion that our time is much superior. But God's definition stands diametrically opposed to ours.

Nebuchadnezzar or Democracy?

We have already dealt with Nebuchadnezzar and our time in chapter 4, yet I think it's needful to take another look at this first and last kingdom. The Bible says the following about the fourth and final kingdom: "And the fourth kingdom shall be strong as iron: forasmuch as iron breaketh in pieces and subdueth all things: and as iron that breaketh all these, shall it break in pieces and bruise" (Daniel 2:40). This is a very negative definition. It looks and acts like a monster; it does no good, only harm. In contrast, Nebuchadnezzar is identified with the words, "thou art this head of gold." The first Gentile government is pictured as the best, while the last government is the worst. That sounds rather strange to us. After all, who would like to live under King Nebuchadnezzar, a man we may consider to be off-balance, an unreasonable, brutal dictator? He had forgotten his dream, but expects his advisers to tell him the dream and interpret it. That is more than unreasonable.

The Iron and Clay Kingdom

Now let's focus our attention on the last kingdom, which consists of iron and clay. Here is what it says in Daniel 2:41-43:

> And whereas thou sawest the feet and toes, part of potters' clay, and part of iron, the kingdom shall be divided; but there shall be in it of the strength of the iron, forasmuch as thou sawest the iron mixed with miry clay. And as the toes of the feet were part of iron, and part of clay, so the kingdom shall be partly strong, and partly broken. And whereas thou sawest iron mixed with miry clay, they shall mingle themselves with the seed of men: but they shall not cleave one to another, even as iron is not mixed with clay.

This is a mixed kingdom; thus the question arises, what does the clay represent? We know that iron represents the Roman power structure—that is a given. Clay is something that does not belong in this structure. It is a foreign material.

I think a clue is found in the words, "they shall mingle themselves with the seed of men." Who are "they"? I propose that Isaiah 64:8 gives us the answer: "But now, O LORD, thou art our father; we are the clay, and thou our potter; and we all are the work of thy hand." We may also read Jeremiah 18:6: "O house of Israel, cannot I do with you as this potter? saith the LORD. Behold, as the clay is in the potter's hand, so are ye in mine hand, O house of Israel." Israel is the clay, and God makes use of it according to His good pleasure.

We already mentioned that God is building the everlasting kingdom, which stands in contrast to all kingdoms and governments of the world in all of human history. This supports our interpretation that the clay represent the Jewish people, who mingle themselves with "the seed of men"; that is, with the Gentiles. The following article describes how rabbis are attempting to reconnect Jews living in Gentile lands (specifically America) with their homeland.

Rabbis work to build ties of U.S. Jews to Israel

As Israel celebrates the 60th anniversary of its creation, Americans are measurably less interested in Israel as they once were, especially those younger than 30. A 2007 survey by the American Jewish Congress (AJC), for example, found that only 69 percent of American Jews said "caring about Israel is a very important part of my being a Jew," compared to 74 percent in 2006 and 79 percent in 2005.

As interest in Israel wanes, American Jewish leaders, especially rabbis, are increasingly concerned. Why are American Jews not feeling a connection to the Jewish state? What can rabbis do to connect Jews to Israel at the synagogues, which, since most American Jewish children attend secular schools, are often the only connecting point for many Jews?

For most American Reform, Conservative and Reconstructionist Jews, aliyah—the mitzvah of moving to Israel or the obligation to move to Israel—is not a top priority.

For the younger generation, said John Rosove, senior rabbi of the Reform Temple Israel of Hollywood, "all they've experienced is the intifada and riots and suicide bombings," and that's why they don't necessarily identify with Israel. Which is why, even though most Jews are concerned about the political situation in Israel and upset by the terrorist attacks against its citizens, many rabbis don't want to emphasize the political situation in Israel because it often doesn't help people connect to the country.

Many rabbis feel that another way to connect Americans to Israel these days is to make sure the relationship isn't only one-way. Rosove pointed out that while Israel is important to the hearts and souls of Jews of the Diaspora, the Conservative and Reform movements can offer Israel a "third way," between "rampant secularism" and "right-wing Orthodoxy" on "what it means to be a Jew there." Rosove says he weaves these themes into many of his sermons and discussions at Temple Israel.

"Sometimes people will say that we're too Israel-oriented," he said. "And I'll say, 'Frankly I don't think we're Israel-oriented enough.'"

-The Jewish Journal, 15 May 2008

Throughout history, the Jews demonstrated their amazing ability to adapt themselves to any culture and custom in the Gentile world. But they remained different; they kept their identity. Although the Jews have been discriminated against and often persecuted and killed, they have lived among the Gentile nations for over two thousand years, without becoming part of them: "they shall not cleave one to another, even as iron is not mixed with clay."

Warning to Believers

Needless to say, this is a warning for the Church of

Jesus Christ. We are in this world, but we are not of it. We as believers should never become part of the identity of the world, regardless of which nation we live in. Iron does not mix with clay, and clay does not mix with iron. To say it in New Testament words, let's read 2 Corinthians 6:14-17:

> Be ye not unequally yoked together with unbelievers: for what fellowship hath righteousness with unrighteousness? and what communion hath light with darkness? And what concord hath Christ with Belial? or what part hath he that believeth with an infidel? And what agreement hath the temple of God with idols? for ye are the temple of the living God; as God hath said, I will dwell in them, and walk in them; and I will be their God, and they shall be my people. Wherefore come out from among them, and be ye separate, saith the Lord, and touch not the unclean thing; and I will receive you.

Throughout history, the Jews demonstrated their amazing ability to adapt themselves to any culture and custom in the Gentile world.

Our desire and future does not lie in any country, but we look for the One to come as Abraham did: "For he looked for a city which hath foundations, whose builder and maker is God" (Hebrews 11:10).

Nebuchadnezzar My Servant

Back to the head of gold. From our point of view, we definitely would consider Nebuchadnezzar's government to be one of the worst. But democracy—where people can participate in an election to determine who rules their nation—we would consider to be the best. We love and respect democracy, and endorse it. We call it the ultimate way of freedom. But God's thoughts stands diametrically opposed to ours.

> *Humanity has progressed to such a high level of sophistication that God has been reduced to a band-aid, a religious tradition that is supposed to undergird and support man's vain ambitions.*

Why did God bestow the title of gold upon Nebuchadnezzar? The answer lies in the fact that Nebuchadnezzar believed God. He recognized the Almighty; he repented and gave the honor to the God of Israel. He testifies of this fact in Daniel 4:37: "Now I Nebuchadnezzar praise and extol and honour the King of heaven, all whose works are truth, and his ways judgment: and those that walk in pride he is able to abase."

God could reveal Himself to this pagan king, and in turn, Nebuchadnezzar recognized the Almighty. Such is definitely not the case any more. Humanity has progressed to such a high level of sophistication that God has been reduced to a band-aid, a religious tradition that is supposed to undergird and support man's vain ambitions. That's why we use the

> *We have created a god who is available to us, for our progress, our prosperity, and our advantages. But it is not the God of the Bible.*

highly respected slogans such as "In God we trust" or "One nation under God." We have created a god who is available to us, for our progress, our prosperity, and our advantages. But it is not the God of the Bible.

Now we should better understand the words of Isaiah 55:8-9: "For my thoughts are not your thoughts, neither are your ways my ways, saith the LORD. For as the heavens are higher than the earth, so are my ways higher than your ways, and my thoughts than your thoughts."

Prosperity and Apostasy

Indeed, God's thoughts are not ours. Blessing, for example, is defined as health, wealth and prosperity. The definition of freedom is interpreted to mean, "I may do as I wish; no one may tell me what to do. I am my own master." Prosperity means having lots of possessions at my disposal for my well-being and enjoyment. These things are the marks of endtime society, even Churchianity—extreme self-centeredness to the extent that we disregard the poor. Self is king!

Self-Love

The Bible identifies the last stages of the end times as the worst. Let's read the first five verses of 2 Timothy 3:

This know also, that in the last days perilous times shall come. For men shall be lovers of their own selves, covetous, boasters, proud, blasphemers, disobedient to parents, unthankful, unholy, Without natural affection, trucebreakers, false accusers, incontinent, fierce, despisers of those that are good, Traitors, heady, highminded, lovers of pleasures more than lovers of God; Having a form of godliness, but denying the power thereof: from such turn away.

> *They are active religious people, but there is one thing wrong: They deny the power of God. What power? The power to cleanse them from the sin of greediness for material possessions.*

We note that this is speaking of "the last days." There is little doubt that we are living in the last stages of the end times. While the last days did begin at the time of our Lord Jesus Christ, we have now arrived at the end stages. During this time in particular, people will be very religious, "having a form of godliness." Religion will prosper. We will learn more on that subject in Part III, titled, "Racing Toward Religious Globalism."

Who are these people who have "a form of godliness"? Are they terrorists, abortionists, communists, socialists, etc.? Obviously not. These people are "Christians"; they apparently love God, but they love pleasure more than God. They go to church. They are active religious people, but there is one thing wrong: They deny the power of God. What power? The power to cleanse them from the sin of greediness for material possessions.

These are religious people indulged in self-esteem, self-love, self-motivation and self-worship. There is no humility and meekness to be found.

What counts is their own well-being, totally disregarding the God of heaven, the Creator of all things. Our society is marked by the "worship" of material possessions instead of the Creator of the materials.

> We arrogantly dismiss the poor and downtrodden with words such as, "They are just too lazy to work; they want everything given to them."

Church Prosperity

Worst of all is that the church is actually immersed in this culture of riches, prosperity and materialism. We think nothing of hoarding more and more for ourselves. We arrogantly dismiss the poor and downtrodden with words such as, "They are just too lazy to work; they want everything given to them." I have yet to read in Scripture where the rich is praised and the poor is condemned. Economic globalism is condemning the poor and worshiping the rich.

The Loss of Riches

When judgment comes upon planet Earth, it will not be accomplished by military force, but will come directly from God. We read the following in Revelation 9:20-21:

> And the rest of the men which were not killed by these plagues yet repented not of the works of their hands, that they should not worship devils, and idols of gold, and silver, and brass, and stone, and of wood: which neither can see, nor hear, nor walk: Neither repented they of their murders, nor of their sorceries, nor of their fornication, nor of their thefts.

They do not repent of their greediness and desire for material things: gold, silver, brass, stone and wood. This is the beast of materialism: accumulation of riches, accumulation of property, and accumulation of possessions. It will be a shocking time when the world

> *It will be a shocking time when the world suddenly realizes that all they have achieved, all they have earned will be lost in just a moment's time.*

suddenly realizes that all they have achieved, all they have earned will be lost in just a moment's time.

Judgment of Prosperity

Here we also need to read Revelation 18, which describes the fall and desolation of Mystery Babylon. "For all nations have drunk of the wine of the wrath of her fornication, and the kings of the earth have committed fornication with her, and the merchants of the earth are waxed rich through the abundance of her delicacies" (verse 3). The religious people, the politicians and the business people are all included. This is global economy, global finances and global merchandise.

When judgment comes, there is no room for repentance:

> The merchants of these things, which were made rich by her, shall stand afar off for the fear of her torment, weeping and wailing, And saying, Alas, alas, that great city, that was clothed in fine linen, and purple, and scarlet, and decked with gold, and precious stones, and pearls! [...] And cried when they saw the smoke of her burning, saying, What city is like unto this great city! And they cast dust on their heads, and cried, weeping and wailing, saying, Alas, alas, that great city, wherein were made rich all that had ships in the sea by reason of her costliness! for in one hour is she made desolate (verses 15-16, 18-19).

It is important to realize that these people who have come under the judgment of God do not express the slightest notion of sorrow and the possibility of repentance. They are devastated only because they have lost everything they had put their trust in: the accumulation of riches.

Global Shockwaves

It seems as if God allows some shockwaves to go through the world economy and the financial system just to remind man that everything could be gone overnight.

Of course, it does not mean that this is the end, in spite of seemingly insurmountable debt, mind-boggling financial losses, increased unemployment and "harder times." The stock market will sooner or later go up, the economy will grow again, and this cycle will continue until the day when God says, "Thus far and no further." The time of reckoning will come, and when it comes, it will be too late.

An Important Question

> *There is no future for this world, there is no hope for America, neither is there hope for any other nation on the face of planet Earth.*

In conclusion of this chapter, permit me to ask some questions. Are you racing toward economic globalism? Does your aim in life consist of accumulating possessions for yourself? Or are you racing toward the completion of the body in Christ? The cardinal question is, Are you part of the spiritual house of God? "Ye also, as lively stones, are built up a spiritual house, an holy priesthood, to offer up spiritual sacrifices, acceptable to God by Jesus Christ" (1 Peter 2:5).

There is no future for this world, there is no hope for America, neither is there hope for any other nation on the face of planet Earth. There is coming a day of reckoning, a day of lamentation, a day of mourning, the day when 2 Corinthians 4:18 becomes reality, "The things which are seen are temporal; but the things which are not seen are eternal."

What are we as believers in Jesus Christ to do in view of these approaching, destructive judgments? Answer: "Wherefore gird up the loins of your mind, be sober, and hope to the end for the grace that is to be brought unto you at the revelation of Jesus Christ" (1 Peter 1:13).

PART III

RACING TOWARD RELIGIOUS GLOBALISM

The last part of this book deals with religious globalism. How is it possible for all religions to unite and to worship the image of the beast? This seems virtually impossible, at least in today's circumstances. But our common sense analysis does not change Scripture. The whole world will worship the dragon, the beast, and the image of the beast. That is an undisputed fact and awaits fulfillment.

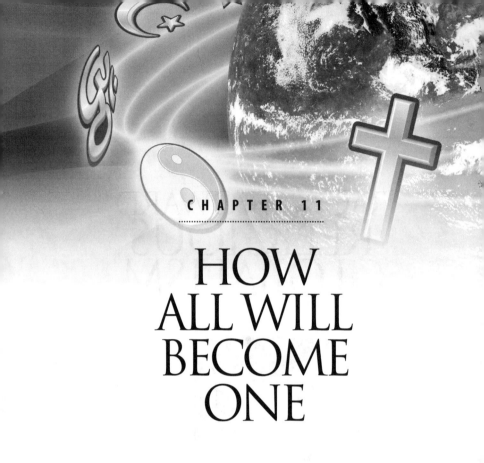

CHAPTER 11

HOW
ALL WILL
BECOME
ONE

Although a truly global world society is in the making, it does not mean that all will lose their identity and fall under one definition. For example, the European Union's motto, "United in Diversity" can be applicable to all of planet Earth. Each nation and religion may keep their identity, but in the end, all will come under the umbrella lead by the dragon, Antichrist and false prophet.

Global Religious Coalition

To reinforce the religious aspect of globalism, let us reread four verses in Revelation 13:

> And they worshipped the dragon which gave power unto the beast: and they worshipped the beast, saying, Who is like unto the beast? who is able to make war with him? [...] And all that dwell upon the earth shall worship him, whose names are not written in the book of life of the Lamb slain from the foundation of the world [...] And he exerciseth all the power of the first beast before him, and causeth the earth and them which dwell therein to worship the first beast, whose deadly wound was healed [...] And he had power to give life unto the image of the beast, that the image of the beast should both speak, and cause that as many as would not worship the image of the beast should be killed (verses 4, 8, 12, 15).

These statements in the four selected verses clearly demonstrate global worship. There is no mention of various religions such as Christianity, Islam, Hinduism, Buddhism, etc. They all worship the dragon, the Antichrist and the image.

Satan's Last Victory

Satan has finally achieved what he set out long ago to do: "I will ascend above the heights of the clouds; I will be like the most High" (Isaiah 14:14). His son is the Antichrist, who receives all power and glory from Satan, the anti-father. This is supported by the false

205

prophet, the anti-holy spirit, and enforced by the image and the mark of the beast.

One can almost hear the hallelujah choruses of victory by the innumerable demons that have attained what they set out to do. Hell is rejoicing!

We already mentioned that the only opposition against the satanic trinity is the saints. But Antichrist made war with the saints and overcame them.

There are others who oppose Antichrist, which is evident from verse 15: "And caused that as many as would not worship the image of the beast should be killed."

Finally, a global religion is established, and people are free to worship in the context of their own religion. But they must also worship the image of the beast. The false prophet has made sure that there will be no detractors, no hiding. There will be total and absolute united global worship.

The Great Imitation

We see again an imitation of the Church of Jesus Christ: she is perfectly united in Him. Jesus prayed, "I in them, and thou in Me, that they may be made perfect in one" (John 17:23). Satan copies the Church. He makes sure all are united in worshiping him.

When the foundation of the Church was laid in Jerusalem, the believers "were of one heart and of one soul" (Acts 4:32). No traitors would be tolerated. When Ananias and Sapphira lied to the Holy Spirit, they instantly died. Here in Revelation 13, those whose heart is not with the Antichrist will be killed: "that as many as would not worship the image of the beast should be killed."

Churchianity

Now comes the big question: How will it be possible for the Antichrist to unite all the religions of the world? The answer is one word: deception!

Churchianity, as we have seen, is well on its way to forming a unified front under the umbrella of the ecumenical movement, the Vatican, the Charismatic movement and the evangelicals, plus many others. This, in spite of extreme diversity within the ranks of Churchianity.

Recently, a pamphlet came to my desk, authored by a Roman Catholic, claiming that there are over 38,000 Protestant denominations in the world. The writer wanted to emphasize the extreme disunity in the Protestant field and offered as a solution a return to the Roman Catholic Church under one shepherd, the pope of Rome.

But to unite these diverse Protestant denominations with the agreed goal to be integrated into the Roman Catholic Church is all but impossible.

There are various major denominations that have a close relationship with the Vatican, and others are in the process of verbalizing an understanding for unity; however, the eradication of the virtually innumerable denominations is definitely out of the question.

What then is the answer in order to fulfill the prophetic Word? Coexistence!

Global Model

We already have a model for the world, and that is the European Union. The uniqueness of this family of nations consists in the fact that they all retain their original identity as nations.

Take, for example, the small country of Estonia, with a population of about 1.3 million. When they joined the European Union, they did not have to surrender their sovereignty. As a matter of fact, the European Union insists that the Estonians speak their language and keep their culture, tradition, customs and holidays.

For this relatively small nation, it would have been easy to change to another language, such as Russian. Already, 30 percent of the Latvian population speaks Russian. According to Wikipedia, over three quarters of the world's scientific literature is published in Russian. In light of that fact, the Estonian language could easily be replaced by the Russian language. The European Union, however, said no to any such proposal. All are respected, all are defended, all are supported, and all are treated equally.

Europe strives to present a united voice to the rest of the world, yet they allow each one to express themselves in their own way. That is unprecedented in history.

What is most unique is that no force is being applied,

no shot is fired. Yet European nations who are not members of the European Union patiently wait in line with application in hand.

Here we have an almost perfect model the world can pattern after to create a union amongst diversity. Each nation can retain its own sovereignty.

United in Diversity

What is happening in the political world is a pattern that is being applied in the religious world.

The new ecumenical philosophy of religion allows each one to retain their original identity. That simply means a Baptist does not need to become a Catholic, neither should we expect a Presbyterian to become a Pentecostal, or a Roman Catholic to become Lutheran. All can retain their own specific identity, yet all become one.

Quite fittingly, the motto of the European Union is "United in diversity." The philosophy of unity in diversity is being practiced throughout Churchianity today. Innumerable movements, conferences and dialogues are taking place continually with the aim to identify each religion's positive aspects and compare it with one another.

Within Churchianity, the Bible is recognized as the authority. Each church denomination, no matter by what name, will point to the Scripture when it comes to identifying their particular doctrine. Thus the new slogan, "Let's agree on the things on which we agree" is becoming a powerful tool to create an understanding amongst Christian religions.

What About Muslims?

Will Muslims be converted to Christianity? Absolutely not! Those who are defenders of their particular religion would rather die than change. Yet the Bible makes it clear, as we have already seen, that the whole world will worship together, and that worship will be directed toward one man, the Antichrist.

At this point of time, the most divisive religion the world has to deal with is Islam. This fact has been highlighted globally because of terrorist activity. There is no denying that most terrorist activities taking place today are sponsored and executed by Muslims. It seems virtually impossible that Muslims could peacefully coexist with Christians, based on the media reports. That may be true on the surface, but in reality, it is not. Muslims, too, will be worshiping with Churchianity, praising Satan's counterfeit messiah, the Antichrist. It's not a question of if, but only when.

Vatican's Response

The Vatican's accommodation of Muslims is documented in the *Catechism of the Catholic Church,* Article 841, under the caption, "The Church's relationship with the Muslims": "The plan of salvation also includes those who acknowledge the Creator, in the first place amongst whom are the Muslims; these profess to hold the faith of Abraham, and together with us they adore the one, merciful God, mankind's judge on the last day" (242-43).

Here we see a clear basis for unity between Islam and Churchianity.

Other Religions

What about other religions? Here again, the Vatican has made provision in Article 842:

> The Church's bond with non-Christian religions is in the first place the common origin and end of the human race: All nations form but one community. This is so because all stem from the one stock which God created to people the entire earth, and also because all share a common destiny, namely God. His providence, evident goodness, and saving designs extend to all against the day when the elect are gathered together in the holy city. (243)

New ways are being paved right now to accommodate all religions of the world under the umbrella of unity, supported and encouraged by various movements and organizations.

How about Hinduism?

We do not need to belabor the point as to the relationship of Hinduism to Churchianity. All one needs to do is to look at the promotional materials of a number of churches and you will find the endorsement of the yoga religion, for example. Other religious-based exercise programs have been fully incorporated into "Christian lands." Besides, Hinduism does not constitute a threat to Churchianity as does Islam, because of its seemingly peaceful nature and practice. Although in recent years the media has reported violence against Christians in India, we have reason to believe that such is the exception and not the rule.

What about Buddhism?

Like Hinduism, Buddhism has made great inroads in nations generally described as Christian.

During a recent shopping mall visit, we found quite an elaborate display of Buddha statutes, incense and other paraphernalia used in religious performance. The fact that this large retail store

> *The false gospel, claiming that all religions are basically good, is winning followers by the millions.*

dedicated significant space to the sale of such religious articles proves beyond a shadow of doubt that Buddhism has successfully infiltrated even the so-called Bible Belt here in the South.

There is no need for war. The integration of foreign religions within Churchianity is well on its way. It is being accomplished in a very peaceful manner and to

212

the temporary benefit of all practitioners.

Unity Worship to Come

The need to change one's religion is unnecessary. "Christians," by whatever name, may keep their identity, and so will the Muslims, Hindus, Buddhists and all others. But in the end, they will unite to fulfill what is written in Revelation 13:4: "And they worshipped the dragon which gave power unto the beast: and they worshipped the beast, saying, Who is like unto the beast? who is able to make war with him?"

The false gospel, claiming that all religions are basically good, is winning followers by the millions. These "believers" have no capacity to distinguish between right and wrong, between the work of God through the Holy Spirit, and the work of Satan through his cunning devices. Why? Because they do not love the truth.

The following article describes Churchianity's growing acceptance of different faiths:

Most US Christians Define Own Theology

A sizable majority of the country's faithful no longer hew closely to orthodox teachings, and look more to themselves than to churches or denominations to define their religious convictions, according to two recent surveys. More than half of all Christians also believe that some non-Christians can get into heaven.

In the Barna survey, 71 percent of American adults say they

are more likely to develop their own set of religious beliefs than to accept a defined set of teachings from a particular church. Even among born-again Christians, 61 percent pick and choose from the beliefs of different denominations. For people under the age of 25, the number rises to 82 percent.

Many "cafeteria Christians" go beyond the teachings of Christian denominations to embrace parts of other world religions.

Half of Americans also believe that Christianity is now just one of many faith options people can choose from (44 percent disagree with that perception). Residents of the Northeast and West were more likely than those in the South and Midwest to say Christianity has lost its status as the favored American religion.

-news.yahoo.com, 14 January 2009

The melting within Christianity is self-evident in this survey. Thus, accepting multiple ways to attain salvation is no longer out of the question. That, however, stands diametrically opposed to the Word of God: "Jesus saith unto him, I am the way, the truth, and the life: no man cometh unto the Father, but by me" (John 14:6).

Merchandiser of Lies

Many of us underestimate our capacity for lying and believing a lie. Take a critical look at what is offered by the merchandiser, and you will quickly realize that many of the statements made are often outright lies. The simple slogan, "Shop and save" is actually a lie, because you can only save if you do not shop.

Take a careful look at some of the delicious food items being offered on television—then go that restaurant, order that food, and you will find there is almost no resemblance between what you saw pictured on your television and the product on your plate. These types of lies are not exceptional; they are accepted as being normal. The whole world is drenched with lies because the world follows the father of lies, the great deceiver.

National Lies

Some time ago, there was an excellent program on public television about America's Midwest. At the end of this fine program, the slogan was proclaimed, "The Midwest feeds, clothes and powers the world." That sounds good to us, especially to those who live in the Midwest, but is this

> Satan, the Antichrist and the false prophet are extremely successful in presenting to the world a lie, and the world will accept it hook, line and sinker.

true? Actually, it is a blatant lie. America's food export is around 10 percent of the total agricultural product. It stands to reason that you can't feed the world with 10 percent of America's agriculture. The simple truth is, the largest agricultural exporter is the continent of Europe, the greatest clothing manufacturer is China, and the biggest power supplier is Saudi Arabia. This statement could only be applicable to the United States, but not to the world.

Lies, no matter how small or great, whether personal or national, are part of Satan's cunning devices and great deception. Satan, the Antichrist and the false prophet are extremely successful in presenting to the world a lie, and the world will accept it hook, line and sinker.

The Image

> And deceiveth them that dwell on the earth by the means of those miracles which he had power to do in the sight of the beast; saying to them that dwell on the earth, that they should make an image to the beast, which had the wound by a sword, and did live. And he had power to give life unto the image of the beast, that the image of the beast should both speak, and cause that as many as would not worship the image of the beast should be killed (Revelation 13:14-15).

This manmade image will be the deciding authority. The image will be able to recognize who and who does not worship the image of the beast. When that time comes, people will finally understand what "freedom of worship" really is. Freedom of worship will be directed toward the image of the beast. All opposition will be eradicated. The Antichrist will have the power to govern planet Earth in a way every politician would like: no opposition.

For additional information, let us quote the following question and answer:

Will all people receive the 666 mark?

No! That number is specifically reserved for the Antichrist; however, a number system divided into two categories will be implemented: 1) The name of the beast and 2) The number of his name. Those who receive the name of the beast are the ones most closely associated with him. They will also worship the image of the beast because they are convinced that he is the Christ.

The second group will receive the number of his name. They, too, are in alliance with the Antichrist. They may not be convinced that he is the real Christ; they have accepted the number for practical purposes.

We may compare this with our Social Security numbers. There are no logical reasons for anyone to refuse a newborn baby his Social Security number. While this may have raised plenty of objections a hundred years ago, today we have grown up with a numbering system and practically all opposition has faded.

Not only do we have Social Security numbers, but there are also many other numbers by which we are identified. To name a few: insurance policies, tax numbers, bank accounts and driver's licenses. You could not exist today if you refused numbers as an identity. However, we must emphasize that the endtime number system will be placed permanently on the right hand or the forehead of every person. That means all the numbers we are identified with today are not the mark of the beast. The name of the beast and the number of his name are still future events.

(119 Most Frequently Asked Questions About Prophecy,
136-37)

Will people voluntarily worship the image of the beast? Based on our understanding of Bible prophecy, the people will gladly accept this final one world religion and unite in worship of this one image. Keep in mind that all opposition is eradicated or diminished. The whole world will agree that Antichrist is the Christ; he is the absolute ruler and is being worshiped by the entire world.

Nebuchadnezzar's Image

We have a prophetic example in the book of Daniel. In chapter 3, we read of King Nebuchadnezzar building a golden image: "Nebuchadnezzar the king made an image of gold, whose height was threescore cubits, and the breadth thereof six cubits: he set it up in the plain of Dura, in the province of Babylon" (verse 1).

What was the purpose? That people should worship his image:

> Then an herald cried aloud, To you it is commanded, O people, nations, and languages, That at what time ye hear the sound of the cornet, flute, harp, sackbut, psaltery, dulcimer, and all kinds of musick, ye fall down and worship the golden image that Nebuchadnezzar the king hath set up: And whoso falleth not down and worshippeth shall the same hour be cast into the midst of a burning fiery furnace (verses 4-6).

No mention is made of freedom of worship. There is no forbidding of any other religion. The people could keep their own idols. That was not the issue. The people of the world had to do one thing to stay alive, and that was to fall down and worship the image.

The Number Six

It is quite interesting to note that the number 6 appears rather frequently. The image was "three score cubits"; that's 60 in height and "six cubits" in breadth. Also the musical instruments listed are 6: cornet, flute, harp, sackbut, psaltery, and dulcimer. Surely this is a prophetic pointer of the epitome of evil, the man whose number is 666.

Three Jews

Only three courageous Jews opposed the worshiping of the image. Their faith in the living God, the God of Israel, caused Nebuchadnezzar in the end to be a great missionary:

> Then Nebuchadnezzar spake, and said, Blessed be the God of Shadrach, Meshach, and Abednego, who hath sent his angel, and delivered his servants that trusted in him, and have changed the king's word, and yielded their bodies, that they might not serve nor worship any god, except their own God. Therefore I make a decree, That every people, nation, and language, which speak any thing amiss against the God of Shadrach, Meshach, and Abednego, shall be cut in pieces, and their houses shall be made a dunghill: because there is no other God that can deliver after this sort (Daniel 3:28-29).

Rejecting the Truth

The Apostle Paul spoke about the coming of Antichrist and gave additional information as to how he is going to implement deception: "Even him, whose coming is after the working of Satan with all power and signs and lying wonders, And with all deceivableness of unrighteousness in them that perish; because they received not the love of the truth, that they might be saved" (2 Thessalonians 2:9-10). Note carefully the words, "they received not the love of the truth." These people who rejected God's free offer of salvation in Jesus Christ now gladly accept the alternative. That is the great deception. Doubtless, these are the people who worship Antichrist and receive the mark of his name.

God Seals Damnation

Next we read something shocking: "And for this cause God shall send them strong delusion, that they should believe a lie" (2 Thessalonians 2:11). Now God gives His seal of approval to the deception, which results in those who refused to believe in Jesus believing a lie. We must also add verse 12: "That they all might be damned who believed not the truth, but had pleasure in unrighteousness." Not believing in Jesus Christ is taking pleasure in unrighteousness.

This is not something we should wait for to happen in the future, because steps toward the implementation of global religion and global worship are in full swing today. That is why we can only shout the warnings with the words of our Lord: "He that hath an ear, let him hear what the Spirit saith unto the churches" (Revelation 2:7).

CHAPTER 12

SATAN'S LAST VICTORY

This chapter is appropriately titled "Satan's Last Victory." He finally achieves what he set out to do ages ago: to be worshiped by man. Anyone who does not worship the image of the beast will be killed. There will be no more ecumenism, no more tolerance and compromise. This is Satan's final offer: Worship the image of the beast or be no more. What Satan does by deception and force, God accomplished through love and grace. In the end, every knee shall bow and every tongue shall confess that Christ is Lord.

Global Satan Worship

"And all that dwell upon the earth shall worship him, whose names are not written in the book of life of the Lamb slain from the foundation of the world" (Revelation 13:8).

This is the documentation that Satan has reached his goal. Humanity is worshiping him and the Antichrist, his visible manifestation on earth. He is now the creator of a "new creation": it is the image of the beast. The false prophet, the imitator of the Holy Spirit, "had power to give life unto the image of the beast." We all know nobody can give life except God, but here something artificial is being created by the fake holy spirit, the false prophet; he "had power to give life."

Again we recognize the mimicking of the Son of God, "And the Word was made flesh, and dwelt among us, (and we beheld his glory, the glory as of the only begotten of the Father,) full of grace and truth" (John 1:14). That is the real thing. The fake is the Antichrist and his propaganda minister, the false prophet.

All Knees Shall Bow

Regarding the worshiping of Antichrist, we note that it says, "All that dwell upon the earth shall worship him." That is utterly amazing. This, too, is the imitation of the real thing. The prophet Isaiah wrote in chapter 45, verse 23 these words: "I have sworn by myself, the word is gone out of my mouth in right-eousness, and shall not return, That unto me every knee shall bow, every tongue shall swear." Later in the New Testament this is confirmed: "That at the name of Jesus every knee should bow, of things in heaven, and things in earth, and things under the earth; And that every tongue should confess that Jesus Christ is Lord, to the glory of God the Father" (Philippians 2:10-11). Interestingly, no exceptions are mentioned. There are no detractors, no one rebels, and no threat of death is made. Also, this is not lim-ited to planet Earth, but also "in heaven." It is uni-versal. This prophecy is yet to be fulfilled.

Christ the Lord Recognized

At the return of Christ, when He comes physically and literally on the Mount of Olives in Jerusalem, several amazing changes will happen.

A topographical change will take place: "And his feet shall stand in that day upon the mount of Olives, which is before Jerusalem on the east, and the mount of Olives shall cleave in the midst thereof toward the east and toward the west, and there shall be a very great valley; and half of the mountain shall remove toward the north, and half of it toward the south" (Zechariah 14:4).

The animal world will change: "The wolf and the lamb shall feed together, and the lion shall eat straw like the bullock: and dust shall be the serpent's meat. They shall not hurt nor destroy in all my holy mountain, saith the LORD" (Isaiah 65:25).

The New Testament also speaks of this change in Romans 8:21-22: "Because the creature itself also shall be delivered from the bondage of corruption into the glorious liberty of the children of God. For we know that the whole creation groaneth and travaileth in pain together until now."

But Not Universal Salvation

The whole world will have to recognize the Supreme Ruler, the Lord Jesus Christ. This statement may be misused by those who teach universal salvation—they teach that in the end everyone will be saved, even Satan. That is far from the truth.

When Jesus comes to earth, He will destroy the visible manifestation of Satan, who has ruled the nations of the world. Jesus Himself will establish the 1,000-year Kingdom of Peace. That does not mean, however, that all are saved who confess that Jesus Christ is Lord. This confession is not unto salvation. This is evident from the state-

> *Jesus Himself will establish the 1,000-year Kingdom of Peace. That does not mean, however, that all are saved who confess that Jesus Christ is Lord.*

ment in Revelation 12:5: "And she brought forth a man child, who was to rule all nations with a rod of iron: and her child was caught up unto God, and to his throne." Those who have been saved by the blood of the Lamb do not need to be ruled with a rod of iron. The opposite is true: he that overcomes will receive "power over the nations" (Revelation 2:26). This speaks not of the believers but of the remnant of humanity who are on planet Earth at the time when Jesus comes back.

> Those who have been saved by the blood of the Lamb do not need to be ruled with a rod of iron.

We should also read verse 20 of Isaiah 65: "There shall be no more thence an infant of days, nor an old man that hath not filled his days: for the child shall die an hundred years old; but the sinner being an hundred years old shall be accursed." This should confirm the fact that the millennium is not populated exclusively by believers. Jesus must rule them with a rod of iron, and those who continue to sin will die or be accursed. This is not heaven; this is happening on planet Earth. Those who violate the law of Christ during the 1,000-year Kingdom of Peace will be eliminated. So at the

> The millennium is not populated exclusively by believers.

end of the 1,000-year Kingdom of Peace, only saints will populate the earth.

Final Confrontation

Then comes the final confrontation against Satan and his demonic host, as recorded for us in Revelation 20. Verse 9 reads: "And they went up on the breadth of the earth, and compassed the camp of the saints about, and the beloved city: and fire came down from God

> *Those who violate the law of Christ during the 1,000-year Kingdom of Peace will be eliminated.*

out of heaven, and devoured them." The new creation will be established: "For, behold, I create new heavens and a new earth: and the former shall not be remembered, nor come into mind" (Isaiah 65:17). The Apostle Peter confirms this in 2 Peter 3:13: "Nevertheless we, according to his promise, look for new heavens and a new earth, wherein dwelleth righteousness."

Worship the Image

In the meantime, Satan continues with his master plan to have all religions of the world worship him. They also worship the Antichrist and the image produced by the world under the authority of the false prophet.

One thing is clear: Deception is the key Satan uses to cause all that dwell upon the earth to worship him. These people have consciously rejected the only name by which they could have been saved. Subsequently, their names are not written in the Book of Life of the Lamb.

Books of Life?

We already discussed the Book of Life in chapter 2, but briefly again, what is the Book of Life? The Book of Life contains every name of every human being ever born. We may call it the ultimate registration book, in which every soul

> *Satan continues with his master plan to have all religions of the world worship him.*

has been recorded. The other book is the Book of Life of the Lamb. Those who have washed their robes in the blood of the Lamb; who have confessed their unworthiness; who have relied completely on the accomplished work of the Lamb of God; and who have become born again of the Spirit of God—they are eternal beings "written in the book of life of the Lamb."

Religious Unity

It stands to reason that all religions—including the non-religious world, the atheists, who claim not to believe—will finally have to worship the image of the beast.

Looking back in history, it seems all but impossible for the nations of the world with their various religions to unite in global worship. But as we have already seen in Parts I and II, "Racing Toward Political Globalism" and "Racing Toward Economic Globalism," this process toward unity is definitely a reality.

Religious Unity in the Works

Let me quote some headlines from the news media to reinforce that religious unity is at work today. *The Bulletin,* 9 July 2008, page 1 carried this headline: "Anglican Bishops Eye Rome," and the subheading says, "There Can Be No Future for Christianity in Europe Without Rome."

L'Osservatore Romano, 20 August 2008, head-lined the Pope's message with these words: "All cultures are waiting for Christ." Christianity without Rome is unthinkable, and Rome, as we have already seen, has plans ready to accommodate all religions of the world.

Tolerance among religious groups is a goal of the world's intellects, politicians and religious leaders—peace at all costs.

Topic, July 2008, writes: "Police of Amsterdam receive Koran instead of the Bible." The article revealed that the police force of Amsterdam must learn to accommodate Muslims. We clearly recognize the spirit of ecumenism, attempting desperately to not only unify the various Christian denominations, but also to accommodate Muslims in this case.

The Bulletin, 24 July 2008, page 1, had this headline: "Pluralism Dominates Americans' Faith." The article reveals that 70% of Americans believe that many religions can lead to eternal life.

These few examples show the tendency of the world today. All religions must unite in order to survive.

Preparation Time Is Ripe

Only a hundred years ago, this was all but impossible. The European world—Europe, America, Australia—was dominated by Churchianity, Asia by Buddhism and Hinduism, while Northern Africa, the Middle East, and the Far East island nations were ruled by Islam. The attempt to unite these religious groups into one was absolutely out of the question.

This was not just because of the diverse faiths alone. There were other reasons, such as transportation and communication, for example. Today, all has drastically changed. Communication is virtually instant with anyone in the world. Transportation time between continents has been reduced to mere hours instead of months. Globalism has brought about a change no one could have dreamed of only a few generations ago.

Globalism's Victory

Today, globalism is irreversible. The world is becoming one, in spite of the many setbacks. There is no stopping the progressive political, economic and religious spirit of our time. One thing is absolutely sure: Revelation 13:4 will be fulfilled: "And they worshipped the dragon which gave power unto the beast: and they worshipped the beast, saying, Who is like unto the beast? who is able to make war with him?"

CHAPTER 13

THE GREATEST TRAGEDY

This last chapter is extremely important because it highlights the great deception within Christianity. The greatest tragedy will be when those who think they have believed and served Christ all their lives, in the end find out it was a false christ. They have been deceived by a false gospel, revealed by a false spirit. All the knowledge in the world and, in this case, Bible prophecy is of no help unless we have individually, fully and unconditionally surrendered to the authority of the Lord Jesus Christ. There is no alternative. Either we are children of God or children of Satan.

The Most Dangerous Religion

Fundamentally speaking, there is little difference between the various religions we have briefly mentioned, and there is no need to research the individual movements. I think there is little if any spiritual gain to be made. One thing we are sure of is that Churchianity is the most dangerous religion. It is the false Church. She looks like the real one, preaches from the Bible, and its members act like true believers, but they are not following Jesus Christ the Crucified One.

> *Churchianity is the most dangerous religion. It is the false Church. She looks like the real one, preaches from the Bible, and its members act like true believers, but they are not following Jesus Christ the Crucified One.*

It is not my intention to identify various denominations, ministries or teachers, of which there are many, who teach contrary to Scripture. Rather, I shall attempt to identify the tendencies of those in our midst who may think they belong to the body of Christ, but are in reality persons whose names are not written in the Book of Life of the Lamb. That is doubtless the greatest danger of all, and will end in the greatest tragedy.

There are people who have heard the Gospel all their lives, participate in church activities, support missionaries, are respectable citizens, do no harm to anyone, basically upright people with high moral standards, yet their names are not written in the Book of Life of the Lamb. Why? Because they have been deceived.

"I Never Knew You"

Here are the words of our Lord Jesus:

> Not every one that saith unto me, Lord, Lord, shall enter into the kingdom of heaven; but he that doeth the will of my Father which is in heaven. Many will say to me in that day, Lord, Lord, have we not prophesied in thy name? and in thy name have cast out devils? and in thy name done many wonderful works? And then will I profess unto them, I never knew you: depart from me, ye that work iniquity (Matthew 7:21-23).

If we are to take this literally, then these people who call the Lord "Lord" are not Hindus, Muslims, Buddhists, atheists, or others—they are "Christians." Actually, they preach the Gospel: "Have we not prophesied in thy name?" They even cast out demons. That is the first sign that legitimized true believers during the establishing period of the Church. In Mark 16:17, Jesus says, "And these signs shall follow them that believe; In my name shall they cast out devils [demons]."

How is it possible that these people's names are not

written in the Book of Life of the Lamb? We have no further information in Scripture about this, but it stands to reason that this is the product of deception.

Jesus warned: "Beware of false prophets, which come to you in sheep's clothing, but inwardly they are ravening wolves" (Matthew 7:15). That means those whose names are not written in the Book of Life of the Lamb are Christians without Christ: they have never been born again to a new creation in Christ.

These people whose names are not written in the Book of Life of the Lamb did more

> *These people were definitely very active Christians. But good works do not determine eternal salvation.*

than just call the Lord "Lord": "...and in thy name [have] done many wonderful works." We have no other details except the words "many" and "wonderful works." This is proof that these people were definitely very active Christians. But good works do not determine eternal salvation.

Let Your Light Shine

What are good works? This is what Jesus has to say: "Let your light so shine before men, that they may see your good works, and glorify your Father which is in heaven" (Matthew 5:16). Note very carefully that the Lord first says, "Let your light so shine." What is your light? It is none other than the presence of the Holy Spirit that you received through the rebirth.

When we believe the Gospel of salvation with all of our hearts, the Holy Spirit seals us for eternity. Ephesians 1:13 reads: "In whom ye also trusted, after that ye heard the word of truth, the gospel of your salvation: in whom also after that ye believed, ye were sealed with that holy Spirit of promise." Now we are light: "Ye are the light of the world," Jesus said.

> *When we believe the Gospel of salvation with all of our hearts, the Holy Spirit seals us for eternity.*

The mistake many of us make is to reinterpret this verse to mean that we are flashlights to shine upon an evil world to expose their sin. But light is what we are, not what we do. Light needs no promotion: it is just there.

Light not only exposes darkness in our surroundings, but it also attracts all kinds of insects, particularly during the night. People who are light will attract those who are in darkness. What is the purpose of your being light? So they, too, may come to the light.

First John 1:7 has this to say: "But if we walk in the light, as he is in the light, we have fellowship one with another, and the blood of Jesus Christ his Son cleanseth us from all sin." Light causes the cleansing blood of Jesus Christ, the Son of God, to be effective for our sins.

What is the result when we let our light shine before men? "That they may see your good works, and glorify your Father

> ✍ *Unfortunately, many of us prefer to show off our works instead of being light.*

which is in heaven" (Matthew 5:16).

This goes against our nature. Unfortunately, many of us prefer to show off our works instead of being light. That is what the people we read of in Matthew 7 did: they advertised their works, but their names are not written in the Book of the Life of the Lamb. There is no need to promote our works, because when people see the Light, they will see our good works also.

Work of Iniquity

Jesus does not answer the question of these people who call Him "Lord, Lord," nor does He debate, but He makes a rather strange statement: "Then will I profess unto them, I never knew you: depart from me, ye that work iniquity" (Matthew 7:23). All the good works these people had done, even in apparent support of Christianity, are judged by the Lord as the "work of iniquity."

From human perspectives, this statement is unreasonable. After all, these people did the best they could according to their ability. They were what we call "good people," trying to do good things. But there was something desperately wrong, and that is revealed with the words, "I never knew you." Jesus identified these people as strangers. They knew Him, because they called Him "Lord, Lord," but Jesus did not know them. This fact reveals another great danger, and that is the assumption that it is sufficient to have knowledge of Jesus, without realizing the requirement that Jesus must know me.

> *They knew Him, because they called Him "Lord, Lord," but Jesus did not know them.*

He Must Know You

Permit me to give you an example. Most of us have at one time or another seen a celebrity, whether politician, athlete or actor. We may have been really close to that person, even shook their hand, or had a picture taken to prove it. So you can rightly say you do know that person. But if you were to ask this celebrity if he knows you, he would most likely say no. Whom does the celebrity know? Only his family, coworkers, and staff; all others are strangers.

Do you belong to the family of God? Then Jesus knows you very personally; He has called you by your name. To Israel, God gave this assurance, "But now thus saith the LORD that created thee, O Jacob, and he that formed thee, O Israel, Fear not: for I have redeemed thee, I have called thee by thy name; thou art mine" (Isaiah 43:1).

Good Works

What are good works, then? They are not the work we do, but the work our Lord can do through us:

> *The Spirit can only work when we cease to do our own works. He can only fill us when we are empty of ourselves.*

"Being confident of this very thing, that he which hath begun a good work in you will perform it until the day of Jesus Christ" (Philippians 1:6). It is the work of the Holy Spirit in our life. But please realize, the Spirit can only work when we cease to do our own works. He can only fill us when we are empty of ourselves. That's the precondition to producing good works.

The Apostle Paul speaks of this work in 1 Corinthians 3:13-15: "Every man's work shall be made manifest: for the day shall declare it, because it shall be revealed by fire; and the fire shall try every man's work of what sort it is. If any man's work abide which he hath built thereupon, he shall receive a

239

reward. If any man's work shall be burned, he shall suffer loss: but he himself shall be saved; yet so as by fire."

Everything and anything we do outside of the Spirit of God will not remain. It will be burned. But what was done through the Holy Spirit in your life "shall receive reward." The alternative to reward is these two words: "suffer loss." This has no relation to eternal salvation, but only to reward.

Positive Gospel

One of the greatest dangers in the process of racing toward religious globalism is the eradication between genuine and fake.

Some time ago, my wife Ruth and I on our travel spent a night at a hotel. During that time, we watched a television program where a famous preacher appeared. I made sure to listen to every word. After the program

> *The possibility that a person becoming a Christian would suffer disadvantage in this world was not part of the message.*

was over, I said to my wife, "This man preached the Bible truthfully. He is not a false teacher and his interpretation was down to earth." But there was one thing that became apparent throughout the program, namely, the positive aspect of the Gospel. The blessings Christ has prepared for them that believe in Him. But the other side of the Gospel was left out. Sin and judgment were not mentioned. Hell and damnation were conveniently excluded, and the possibility that a person becoming a Christian would suffer disadvantage in this world was not part of the message. That is a dangerous gospel. It does not represent the whole truth of God's plan of salvation.

Negative Gospel

Let's take a look at the negative, but true gospel: "Blessed are ye, when men shall revile you, and persecute you, and shall say all manner of evil against you falsely, for my sake" (Matthew 5:11). How about John 15:20? "Remember the word that I said unto you, The servant is not greater than his lord. If they have persecuted me, they will also persecute you; if they have kept my saying, they will keep yours also." What Jesus says in Matthew 16:24 is definitely not very positive: "Then said Jesus unto his disciples, If any man will come after me, let him deny himself, and take up his cross, and follow me."

Paul's Disadvantage

The Apostle Paul is an example for the Church. Before he became a Christian, he was a respected, highly educated and well-to-do man in his community. But after he became a believer in the Lord Jesus Christ, he testifies: "But in all things approving ourselves as the ministers of God, in much patience, in afflictions, in necessities, in distresses, In stripes, in imprisonments, in tumults, in labors, in watchings, in fastings" (2 Corinthians 6:4-5). That's not very positive.

Further, in 2 Corinthians 11:23-27 he testifies:

> Are they ministers of Christ? (I speak as a fool) I am more; in labours more abundant, in stripes above measure, in prisons more frequent, in deaths oft. Of the Jews five times received I forty stripes save one. Thrice was I beaten with rods, once was I stoned, thrice I suffered shipwreck, a night and a day I have been in the deep; In journeyings often, in perils of waters, in perils of robbers, in perils by mine own countrymen, in perils by the heathen, in perils in the city, in perils in the wilderness, in perils in the sea, in perils among false brethren; In weariness and painfulness, in watchings often, in hunger and thirst, in fastings often, in cold and nakedness.

> *If success, blessings and prosperity are the guideline, then the Apostle Paul certainly made a mistake in refusing to accept promotion of his gospel messages.*

That is the other side of the cross, and it is part of the Gospel.

A Positive Deception

If success, blessings and prosperity are the guideline, then the Apostle Paul certainly made a mistake in refusing to accept promotion of his gospel messages by someone who was not a believer:

> And it came to pass, as we went to prayer, a certain damsel possessed with a spirit of divination met us, which brought her masters much gain by soothsaying: The same followed Paul and us, and cried, saying, These men are the servants of the most high God, which shew unto us the way of salvation. And this did she many days. But Paul, being grieved, turned and said to the spirit, I command thee in the name of Jesus Christ to come out of her. And he came out the same hour (Acts 16:16-18).

> *We can't deny this was a welcome promotion for the preaching of the Gospel. But Paul, who walked in the Light, recognized the work of darkness.*

We note this unnamed damsel, possessed with a spirit of divination, did tell the truth, "These men are the servants of the most high God, which shew unto us the way of salvation." We can't deny this was a welcome promotion for the preaching of the Gospel. But Paul, who walked in the Light, recognized the work of darkness. The demon was cast out. No more promotion for the Gospel. What was the result?

> As far as economy and finances are concerned, the Christianized nations virtually monopolize planet Earth.

"And the multitude rose up together against them: and the magistrates rent off their clothes, and commanded to beat them. And when they had laid many stripes upon them, they cast them into prison, charging the jailor to keep them safely" (Acts 16:22-23). They were beaten bloody and cast into prison. That was not a very positive aspect of the Gospel of Jesus Christ. But it is part of the Gospel of our salvation.

European Dominion

Churchianity as a religion is not only the largest religion in the world, but also the most powerful. Churchianity has a dominating imprint on the world. When it comes to culture and influence, the Church is second to none. As far as economy and finances are concerned, the Christianized nations virtually monopolize planet Earth.

Churchianity as a political, cultural and religious influence, was established by Rome, and from there spread across Europe and the rest of the world.

Christianized Europe went all over the world establishing colonies and literally dividing the world into nations and sub-nations. During the colonial and post-colonial times, the Christianized nations of Europe forced a degree of Christian culture upon the world. Thus, the world's five continents were influenced by Roman (European) languages, religion, business practices

> *Churchianity as a political, cultural and religious influence, was established by Rome, and from there spread across Europe and the rest of the world.*

and democracy. Therefore, only Christianized Europe with its diverse culture, languages and customs is capable of unifying the world and creating a truly global religion acceptable to all people on earth.

I believe it is for that reason the Bible does not mention other nations except Israel, their neighbors in the Middle East and Europe. Rome, according to Scripture, is the last Gentile superpower, and in the end all nations will have to follow the model they have established in the past and will institute in the future.

So when we speak of racing toward religious globalism, we are right on track when we analyze Europe and Churchianity in the light of Bible prophecy.

Antichrist Versus Christ

The devil, who is also called the father of lies, is

the great imitator of the God of heaven; thus, he is forced to imitate a coming kingdom Christ. From Scripture we know that Christ will rule the nations, "And she brought forth a man child, who was to rule all nations with a rod of iron: and her child was caught up unto God, and to his throne" (Revelation 12:5). Antichrist, on the other hand, will rule the world by deception. This is necessary because he is a defeated foe; he cannot challenge God openly.

In Revelation we see the Lamb of God magnified, not by force or deception, but by truth and light:

> And hast made us unto our God kings and priests: and we shall reign on the earth. And I beheld, and I heard the voice of many angels round about the throne and the beasts and the elders: and the number of them was ten thousand times ten thousand, and thousands of thousands; Saying with a loud voice, Worthy is the Lamb that was slain to receive power, and riches, and wisdom, and strength, and honour, and glory, and blessing. And every creature which is in heaven, and on the earth, and under the earth, and such as are in the sea, and all that are in them, heard I saying, Blessing, and honour, and glory, and power, be unto him that sitteth upon the throne, and unto the Lamb for ever and ever. And the four beasts said, Amen. And the four and twenty elders fell down and worshipped him that liveth for ever and ever (Revelation 5:10-14).

This is true heavenly worship, recognizing that to

the Lamb of God belong all attributes of glory.

Self-Exaltation

Contrary to the Lamb of God, the Antichrist exalts himself. This is documented in 2 Thessalonians 2:4, "Who opposeth and exalteth himself above all that is called God, or that is worshipped; so that he as God sitteth in the temple of God, shewing himself that he is God." Here we have the great imitation. Notice the word *himself* appears twice in this verse. He takes it upon himself. Jesus, the Lamb of God, receives the glory from those He has purchased with His own blood. That is the distinct difference between our Lord Jesus Christ and the defeated foe, the devil.

Therefore, in the end it boils down to two groups we already spoke of in the beginning: the ones whose names are not written in the Lamb's Book of Life, and those whose names are written in the Lamb's Book of Life, who were purchased with the blood of Christ.

> *The Lamb of God receives the glory from those He has purchased with His own blood.*

Another Jesus, Another Spirit, Another Gospel

In order for Satan to fulfill his plan, he must have Churchianity on his side. Only Churchianity is capable of uniting the world to form a truly religious globalism.

But there is one problem: the real Church consisting of born-again believers. They are the hindering element for the devil to implement religious globalism.

Satan therefore has to influence the Church and cause confusion to such an extent that it becomes virtually impossible to distinguish between a real Christian and one that is fake. In other words, he has to mimic Jesus, the Holy Spirit and the Gospel.

> *Only Churchianity is capable of uniting the world to form a truly religious globalism.*

Here is what the apostle Paul writes, inspired by the Holy Spirit, "For if he that cometh preacheth another Jesus, whom we have not preached, or if ye receive another spirit, which ye have not received, or another gospel, which ye have not accepted, ye might well bear with him" (2 Corinthians 11:4). This fake Jesus must look almost identical to the real one. This spirit must mimic the Spirit of God. That is the key to the successful preaching of "another gospel."

Apparently, many believers in the Corinthian Church did not have the spiritual capacity to distinguish between the real and the false Gospel.

How far the imitation has progressed can be seen from the following article:

Charter for Religious Harmony

A website launched with the backing of technology industry and Hollywood elite urges people worldwide to help craft a framework for harmony between all religions.

The Charter for Compassion project on the internet at www.charterforcompassion.org springs from a "wish" granted this year to religious scholar Karen Armstrong at a premier Technology, Entertainment and Design (TED) conference in California.

"Tedizens" include Google founders Larry Page and Sergey Brin along with other Internet icons as well as celebrities such as Forest Whittaker and Cameron Diaz.

Wishes granted at TED envision ways to better the world and come with a promise that Tedizens will lend their clout and capabilities to making them come true.

Armstrong's wish is to combine universal principles of respect and compassion into a charter based on a "golden rule" she believes is at the core of every major religion.

The Golden Rule essentially calls on people to do unto others as they would have done unto them.

"The chief task of our time is to build a global society where people of all persuasions can live together in peace and harmony," Armstrong said.

"If we do not achieve this, it seems unlikely that we will have a viable world to hand on to the next generation."

Charter for Compassion invites people from "all faiths, nationalities, languages and backgrounds" to help draft statements of principles and actions that should be taken.

(Copyright AFP 2008)

-*www.breitbart.com,* 14 November 2008

In answer to that article, the following commentary:

> The "Charter for Religious Harmony" already exists: "And they worshipped the dragon which gave power unto the beast: and they worshipped the beast, saying, Who is like unto the beast? who is able to make war with him? [...] And all that dwell upon the earth shall worship him, whose names are not written in the book of life of the Lamb slain from the foundation of the world [...] And he exerciseth all the power of the first beast before him, and causeth the earth and them which dwell therein to worship the first beast, whose deadly wound was healed [...] And he had power to give life unto the image of the beast, that the image of the beast should both speak, and cause that as many as would not worship the image of the beast should be killed" (Revelation 13:4, 8, 12, 15).

> (*Midnight Call,* April 2009, pg. 33)

The Mark of Another Gospel

This is an extremely important issue. Let us read Galatians 1:6-9:

> I marvel that ye are so soon removed from him that called you into the grace of Christ unto another gospel: Which is not another; but there be some that trouble you, and would pervert the gospel of Christ. But though we, or an angel from heaven, preach any other gospel unto you than that which we

have preached unto you, let him be accursed. As we said before, so say I now again, If any man preach any other gospel unto you than that ye have received, let him be accursed.

Very clearly, this speaks of another gospel. That, incidentally, is a mark of a false teaching. It is of the most dangerous kind. What is that mark? The insistence of placing another book, message or new revelation beside the Bible, in its fundamental teachings. Such extra-biblical revelation is claimed to be the ultimate authority, the key to understanding the Gospel. That is another gospel. It is the false Gospel.

There are many "other gospels." Paul identifies one specific ingredient by which we can recognize that it is the true Gospel: "For do I now per-

> *When Satan is successful in having an alternative gospel preached to the church at large, then Churchianity will be led astray and will follow this deceptive gospel away from the cross.*

suade men, or God? or do I seek to please men? for if I yet pleased men, I should not be the servant of Christ" (Galatians 1:10). What does it mean, "to please man?" It is the opposition to pleasing Christ. That is the offense of the cross. When Satan is successful in having an alternative gospel ("other gospel") preached to the church at large, then

Churchianity will be led astray and will follow this deceptive gospel away from the cross.

Alternative Gospel

This is a new gospel, a slightly altered one. It targets self instead of Jesus Christ and Him crucified. Such a gospel is now being successfully preached all over the world. This gospel is more acceptable to a larger audience and less offensive to anyone who does not believe the Gospel of the cross. This altered gospel is the perfect tool to unite Churchianity into a solid, religious movement, which becomes stronger as time goes by.

Realizing that Churchianity is already the largest and most powerful religion on planet Earth, and considering that the Protestant branch would come to an agreement with the Roman Catholic Church and form one powerful united Christian church under the umbrella of the Vatican, then we have the recipe for a religious power structure to virtually control planet Earth.

Final Global Worship

Other religions, as we already mentioned, can be accommodated more quickly because the new Gospel is not built on the unmovable Rock of Salvation. What is the end result? "And all that dwell upon the earth shall worship him [Antichrist]."

The alternative gospel is very appealing and pleasant to the natural person. It requires you to be agreeable and tolerant, and not to speak about sin, the devil, hell, death and destruction. The new gospel is pleasant to the ear, but it stands in direct opposition to the real gospel revealed in the Word of God: "For the word of God is quick, and powerful, and sharper than any twoedged sword, piercing even to the dividing asunder of soul and spirit, and of the joints and marrow, and is a discerner of the thoughts and intents of the heart" (Hebrews 4:12).

Only the Word of God is capable of dividing soul and spirit: that means the things that are natural to man, and the things that are spiritual, which belong to God. It is the discerner of things we have not yet thought about. When we permit the Word of God, the "twoedged sword" to pierce our life, it will result in a radical division between the things we possess and what we are, between our plans and God's plan for us.

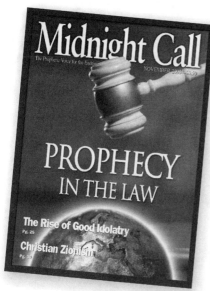